Managing Difficult Behaviour

A handbook for foster carers of the under 12s

Clare Pallett, Kathy Blackeby, Caroline Bengo,
William Yule, Roger Weissman and Stephen Scott
with **Eileen Fursland**

Published by CoramBAAF Adoption and Fostering Academy
41 Brunswick Square
London WC1N 1AZ
www.corambaaf.org.uk

Coram Academy Limited, registered as a company limited by guarantee in England and Wales number 9697712, part of the Coram group, charity number 312278

First published by BAAF in 2008 978 1 905664 27 6

This edition published by CoramBAAF in 2015

British Library Cataloguing in Publication Data
A catalogue record for this book is available from the British Library

ISBN 978 1 910039 36 6

Project management by Shaila Shah, Director of Publications, CoramBAAF
All cartoons by Fran Orford
Designed and typeset by Helen Joubert Design
Printed in Great Britain by The Lavenham Press
Trade distribution by Turnaround Publisher Services, Unit 3, Olympia Trading Estate, Coburg Road, London N22 6TZ

Contents

Acknowledgements

There are a whole host of colleagues and practitioners whose work in the field of parent training informed and inspired the development of the *Fostering Changes* programme and consequently, this guide. In particular, we would like to thank Carolyn Webster-Stratton, The Centre for Fun and Families, Matt Sanders and the Triple P Positive Parenting Programme and Rex Forehand and Robert MacMahon.

Special thanks go to Eileen Fursland who has taken the ideas and materials from the *Fostering Changes* training programme and adapted these for direct use by foster carers. She has done this with refreshing clarity, humour and directness. And finally, thanks to Fran Orford for his cartoons, which are both humorous and thought-provoking.

Notes about the authors

The Fostering Changes author team

The original edition of *Fostering Changes*, on which this handbook draws, was authored by Clare Pallett, Kathy Blackeby, William Yule, Roger Weissman and Stephen Scott and published by BAAF in 2005. Subsequent editions have been added to by Karen Bachmann, Caroline Bengo, Kirsty Slack, Matt Woolgar and Hilary Lawson, and published in 2011 and then again in 2014. Caroline Bengo and Kathy Blackeby have been most involved in the revision of this edition of *Managing Difficult Behaviour*, which draws on the 2014 edition of *Fostering Changes*.

Caroline Bengo is a qualified social worker with over 20 years' experience of working in both statutory and voluntary sectors. She has specialised in working with Looked After Children (LAC) and young people since 1999. As a social worker and clinical specialist, Caroline has specialised in supporting foster and adoptive families through the unique and challenging journeys they face, working therapeutically, providing evidence-based interventions, direct work and family work. As a trainer, Caroline is experienced in facilitating parenting groups for birth, foster and adoptive families.

Kathy Blackeby is a social worker with extensive experience of working in child and adolescent mental health both in the community and with the Conduct, Adoption and Fostering Team at the Maudsley Hospital. She works as clinical specialist as well as being a supervisor on the IAPT parent training scheme. Kathy is a trainer who has facilitated family partnership training, the Fostering Changes programme and the facilitators' course.

Freelance writer

Eileen Fursland is a freelance writer specialising in issues affecting children and young people. She has written extensively for BAAF, as well as for a range of other organisations, newspapers and magazines, including *Children & Young People Now*. Eileen's publications for BAAF include her books *Facing up to Facebook* (2nd edition 2013); *Social Networking and Contact* (2010); *Foster Care and Social Networking* (2011); and a booklet for young people, *Social Networking and You* (3rd edition 2015). She has also co-authored *Preparing to Adopt: A training pack for preparation groups in England* (2014), with Elaine Dibben and Nicky Probert.

Cartoonist

Fran Orford's cartoons have been used in over 70 magazines and newspapers in both the UK and abroad, including *The Observer*, *Private Eye* and *The Telegraph*. Before becoming a cartoonist Fran set up and ran a Leaving Care Team for NCH in Halifax, West Yorkshire, and before that he worked with homeless and disadvantaged teenagers in London.

A note about 'Fostering Changes: How to improve relationships and manage difficult behaviour'

Caring for looked after children can be an immensely stressful and complex task and foster carers need opportunities to process their experiences and reflect on their thoughts and feelings. The *Fostering Changes* Programme was first set up in 1999 at the Maudsley Hospital, London, to provide practical advice and skills-based training for foster carers in order to develop their skills in managing difficult and challenging child behaviour and forming positive relationships with the children whom they look after, and the programme was first published in 2008. Since then, it has been considerably developed and a new edition was published by BAAF in 2014.

This unique handbook, *Managing Difficult Behaviour*, has been developed from that training programme and is designed for use with foster carers in the local authority and voluntary and independent sectors. Many of the ideas and strategies are used in parent training programmes that use a cognitive behavioural approach to work with parents in order to develop their skills. The course has been evaluated and the evidence has shown significant improvements in carer–child interaction, specific child problems causing most worry to carers, and child emotional symptoms. It has also demonstrated a beneficial effect on carers' sense of confidence and self-efficacy.

By reading this handbook, foster carers will be able to acquaint themselves with some of the techniques suggested in the training programme, but reading the handbook on its own is not the same as actually attending a training course, in which the learning, group work, homework, skills practice and continuous evaluation result in a different experiential learning, which this handbook cannot entirely provide on its own. However, this handbook will give you a good flavour of the ideas and approaches used in training and provide clear guidance and advice on a number of different strategies to try out with the children in your care. These are designed to help you feel more calm and confident and to facilitate positive changes in the ways your child thinks, feels and behaves.

Is this programme for you?

As a foster carer, you are with your child every day and you are an important person in his life – so you are the one who can do most to help improve his behaviour and boost his self-esteem.

Here's some questions to ask yourself.

- **Would you like to develop a better relationship with the child you are caring for? Yes/No**
- **Do you feel you are constantly nagging your child? Yes/No**
- **Do you sometimes struggle to deal with his tantrums, rudeness or aggression? Yes/No**
- **Do you sometimes wish you felt more warmly towards him? Yes/No**
- **Does he have a low opinion of himself? Yes/No**
- **Does he sometimes wind you up until you feel desperate or at the end of your tether? Yes/No**
- **Do you sometimes feel powerless when you want to get him to do something? Yes/No**
- **Do you often find things he does irritating or annoying? Yes/No**
- **Does he often play up to get your attention? Yes/No**
- **Does he seem to find it impossible to concentrate or get on with things on his own? Yes/No**

If you answered "yes" to several (or all) of these questions, this book is for you. It will give you new skills that will help you to improve your child's behaviour. The techniques and strategies you learn will help you achieve a more positive relationship with your child and a more harmonious family life. Learning to behave well will also make your child feel better about himself.

Developed by experts, tried and tested by carers

This book is based on a training programme for foster carers looking after children with challenging behaviour, called *Fostering Changes*. The training programme was set up in 1999 at the Maudsley Hospital, London, by a group of experienced clinicians in adoption and fostering and child psychology and psychiatry. It is now mandatory training in a number of local authorities across England, and has also been used successfully elsewhere in the UK, and will be rolled out in Wales in 2015–16.

The training programme is based on the well-established principles of social learning theory, and targets patterns of behaving, relating and thinking. Parenting training programmes based on these techniques, delivered in a structured way over several weeks, have been found to be the single most effective way of treating behaviour problems in children.

The results of the *Fostering Changes* training programme have been outstanding.

Many of the carers who have completed the programme are delighted with the changes they have managed to make. The evidence has shown significant improvements in the interactions between carers and children as well as in the children's problem behaviours and emotional symptoms. Learning the new skills has also helped carers feel more confident and competent.

'Life is so much better for all of us'

Sally had been fostering six-year-old twins, a boy and a girl, for nine months when she went on the Fostering Changes course.

'Charlie had very challenging behaviour. He was aggressive, would lash out, smash up his room and destroy things. He would do this not only at times when he was angry or anxious but just out of the blue – he would snap a pair of sunglasses, for instance, or run something under the tap to spoil it. He had no sense of danger and would dash out into the road and run up and down the aisles in the supermarket.

'Rosie was very guarded and would become very tearful at the slightest thing. She would say that she hated herself, that she's not a nice person. Even something as small as my saying it was too late for a bedtime story would be enough to start the tears and she would say distressing things like: "I wish I was dead".

'But the strategies I learned on the course certainly worked for these two. I was surprised at the effect it has had.'

Charlie's behaviour had been a big issue but once Sally had learned how to manage it, everything changed – and she felt able to adopt the twins.

'Charlie's behaviour has gone from being the worst you could think of to just really occasional instances. Children can be as adorable as you like, but their challenging behaviour could make you think: "I can't handle that" – which would have been such a shame for Charlie and Rosie. Since going on the course, life for all of us has been so much better.'

Learn how to help your child behave well

If you can take part in a *Fostering Changes* training programme, this book will act as a reminder and back-up for you once the course is over. If you can't attend the training in person, this book will allow you to work through much of the programme at home on your own. It explains the techniques and strategies and provides training exercises that will help you to develop a range of skills in managing behaviour.

Being a good foster carer demands many of the same qualities as being a good parent, but of course there are big differences: you are working in a different context, with children with very different needs. However, the social learning techniques and strategies in this book can be used in any family situation and with all children. They are consistent with the positive approach to discipline that fostering agencies advocate.

The programme set out in the book won't provide you with all the answers – there are no "right answers" when dealing with the infinite variety of ways that troubled children express their frustration, anger, stress and insecurity. However, it will provide you with ways in which you can help your child, in your own way, in your own home.

These techniques and strategies are not difficult to understand or to put into practice. They will help you to build positive bonds with your child and to encourage good behaviour, set limits and apply discipline. The improvements in your relationship and in your child's behaviour will make every day easier and more enjoyable not only for him, but also for you and the rest of your family.

And in the long term, helping your child learn to behave more appropriately could transform his life.

'It was really helpful'

Heather was fostering a three-year-old girl with severe behaviour problems.

'As a foster carer, you go on lots of courses and although you hope they will be useful you often think, "It's just another course". But the Fostering Changes *course was really helpful. Her problem behaviour didn't stop altogether but in the end she changed.'*

Looking at behaviour

Looked after children are a diverse group, with a great variety of needs. These children have widely different personal, social, ethnic and religious backgrounds, and diverse experiences of family and community life, and all of these factors must be considered by the social workers and foster carers looking after them. But one common point is that many of these children will have been damaged by their early life experiences and may consequently have high levels of social, physical, educational and mental health difficulties; fostering them is therefore a complex, stressful task. These children may be depressed, anxious, chronically lacking in confidence, and have poor social skills. They may also behave aggressively, be withdrawn, destructive, impulsive and out of control. Children presenting such behaviours can represent a challenge even for the most dedicated, skilled and experienced foster carers.

Sometimes, children's problems are not so serious, yet daily life with them can still be wearing because they demand constant attention or reassurance or have developed irritating, antisocial habits.

Which behaviour would you like to tackle?

The first step in tackling difficult behaviour is to be clear about what the child is actually doing. It's easy to say something sweeping, like 'He's lazy' or 'She's disobedient'. However, in order to change things, you need to be more precise. For example: 'He lies on the sofa and watches television while the rest of us are clearing up after supper' or 'When I tell her to stop doing something, she ignores me'.

If you can identify the behaviour quite precisely, it is easier to decide the best way to change it. It's also easier to recognise improvements when they occur. This programme will introduce you to a number of different strategies you can use to change your child's behaviour.

Rate the three main problems

What are your main concerns about the child you are looking after? List the three problem behaviours that you would most like to reduce.

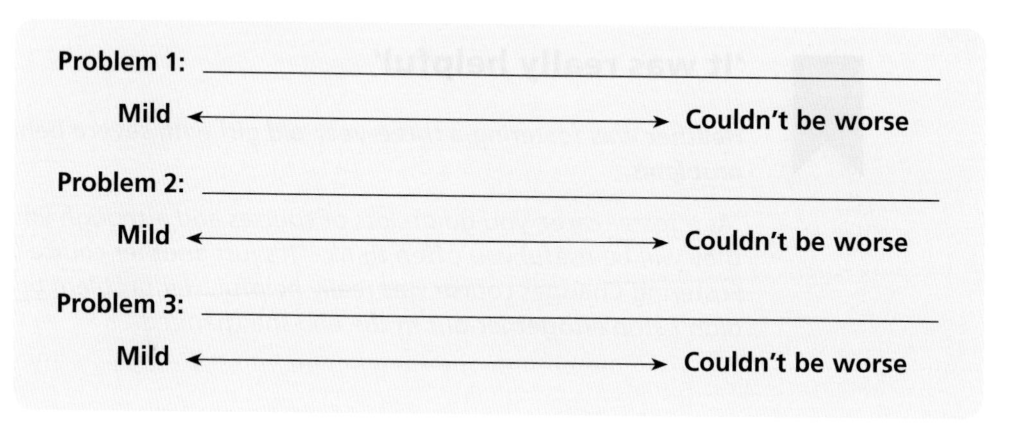

If you are willing to work through the exercises in each chapter of this book, think about what you have learned and put it into practice with determination and perseverance; you will soon have several new and effective ways to tackle these and other problems.

1 Why do children behave the way they do?

In response to the way adults in their lives treat them, children develop certain ways of behaving and relating to people and certain beliefs and feelings about themselves.

So when a child comes to you and some of the things she does and says surprise you, you need to think about how she might have learned these things in the first place.

Many children coming into foster care have experienced neglect and/or serious physical and/or emotional abuse, loss and trauma. Many of them have mental health problems or behaviour disorders. Due to the difficult start they have had or the way adults in their lives have treated them, many of these children either "can't behave" or "won't behave". In other words, they have developed behaviour patterns that allowed them to survive in a situation of neglect or abuse, but which are not appropriate in normal family life, school and other social situations.

Experiences of looked after children

Most looked after children have had difficult experiences. They may have experienced neglect and/or physical, emotional or sexual abuse. They may have had parents with substance abuse or mental health problems and they may have witnessed domestic violence. They have been separated from their family, they may have been moved several times and they are likely to feel great uncertainty about their future.

Experiencing this kind of stress and early experiences can have a long-term impact on a child's developing brain and physiology. The impact of this can start very early on.

Babies are totally dependent on their relationship with their caregiver for their survival. Without an adult who is committed to care for them, they could die. So it is vital for babies to have a secure attachment relationship that is safe and nurturing. A good attachment experience with a carer who is closely attuned to her needs is extremely important for the baby to develop feelings of trust and security.

If care is not forthcoming or it is erratic, the baby's needs go unmet and so the baby may not develop effective strategies to regulate stress.

Some children do develop the ability to regulate stress in babyhood but then, at a stage when they are able to process their feelings, they are exposed to terrifying events. They may be threatened or fear for their lives or see someone close to them threatened or beaten, for example. Such events can lead to post-traumatic stress disorder (PTSD).

Childhood maltreatment, trauma and neglect can have a long-lasting impact on cognitive functions, such as learning and memory, on all major bodily systems, and on emotional and social functioning. In time, the child may adapt to these impacts, but adapting can lead to behaviours and other symptoms of disorder that can be puzzling to other people.

Every aspect of her life may be variously affected – including her behaviour, how she manages her emotions, her ability to learn and her ability to understand, empathise with and interact with other people and form attachments. Some children may have difficulties (emotional, cognitive and social) from their early experiences for which they may require specialist assessment and help, for example, from Child and Adolescent Mental Health Services (CAMHS).

How might early adverse experiences affect a child's behaviour?

The neglected child

- Possible behaviours include eating disorders, stealing food, inability to accept care, insistent demanding of attention or an inability to accept attention, compulsive self-reliance, inability to attend to personal hygiene even when the opportunity is there. The child may be destructive or particularly acquisitive of possessions.

The emotionally abused child

- Possible behaviours include stealing, lying, having restricted empathy or conscience for hurt done to others and/or having significant difficulties making relationships with peers or adults.

The physically abused child

- Typical behaviours include being either overly fearful and anxious. They may also have learned to be aggressive, for example, bullying or being cruel to animals.

The sexually abused child

- Some typical behaviours would include soiling, wetting, making inappropriate sexual overtures, offering indiscriminate affection, having fears and phobias, for instance, about getting changed or getting into the bath, excessive masturbation, being "rude", and being fearful of relationships.

The child affected by parental substance misuse

- Children often fail to thrive and have behavioural, cognitive and other psychological difficulties. They are likely to have experienced neglect and/or abuse of various kinds as detailed above.

The child affected by domestic violence

- Babies may be physically affected even while in the womb, if the mother is extremely stressed. Children who have witnessed domestic violence may still remain fearful, even when living with new carers where there is no violence and indeed their expectation may be that violence occurs without them seeing it.

Resilience

Each child is unique. It's impossible to predict the way their early experiences will affect the way they develop and behave in the future.

There are many factors that come into play to determine how early experiences will affect a particular child. Some children do surprisingly well, given what they have been through, while others, who may appear to have suffered less severe maltreatment, may struggle more. In other words, some children seem to be more "resilient" than others.

Robbie Gilligan, Professor of Social Work and Social Policy at Trinity College, Dublin, defines resilience as:

...the qualities which cushion a vulnerable child from the worst effects of adversity in whatever form it takes and which may help a child or young person to cope, survive and even thrive in the face of great hurt or disadvantage.

(Gilligan, 1997, p12)

What makes for resilience is a complex picture and still not fully understood. Some of the qualities that help foster resilience include:

- Social skills

- Education
- Friendships
- Talents and interests
- Positive values

We do know that the right skills, support, input and belief from their foster carer make a difference to children's lives.

Developmental stages

Children's development is sometimes seen as a series of "stages" – you often read about these in baby books and child care manuals. At each stage there are certain things a child of a particular age might be expected to do, for example, physical abilities such as crawling or walking, holding a pencil or using a knife and fork, and to understand language and to start talking. There are also social skills that children develop as they grow older, for example, they learn how to play, share and take turns with other children and to understand what they might be thinking and feeling. The idea of "developmental stages" can be a helpful general guide, but the development of different skills, emotions and behaviours is not always straightforward, particularly when children have had a difficult start in life.

Developmental stages should not be seen as set in stone. Some children will develop more quickly, others more slowly. A child's level of ability in one area of development might not match with a similar level in another; for example, an eight-year-old may be very articulate in arguing with her friends about the rules of a game, but fail to understand how these arguments made her parents or carers feel. A child might have taken responsibility for caring for younger siblings but be unable to look after her own needs.

Sometimes, when a child has suffered a great upheaval in their life, the behaviours that they have most recently acquired may be the most vulnerable to disruption. If this happens, the child might rely on earlier types of behaviour, the kind of behaviour she showed when she was younger, such as expecting an adult to get her washed and dressed. She still has the skills she has most recently mastered – getting washed and dressed by herself but, in the face of the stress she is experiencing, she finds it harder to present these newer skills consistently, so she falls back on those she has more confidence in.

So how should you respond if a child is showing these "younger" behaviours? It's best if you can accept and understand them as a sign that the child is going through a period of stress, and don't put her under pressure to use her age-appropriate skills. She has not lost these skills – and, in time, you can sensitively encourage her to start using them again.

What causes behaviour problems?

This book will help you work out how you can change children's behaviour for the better. Later in this chapter we will look at the immediate and longer-term triggers for particular behaviours and what you can do on a day-to-day basis to help the child behave better.

As well as changing a child's difficult behaviour, it's important to try to **understand** it and to recognise the wider context and the factors that might lie behind it. For example, refusing to sit at the dinner table to eat a meal looks like bad behaviour – but children who have never been taught by their parents to do these things can't really be expected to take to them straight away when they move to a foster home. A child may refuse to try anything new or join in with family activities – but if, in her birth family, she has always been humiliated or belittled for failing or told she's no good at anything, her self-esteem will be at rock-bottom, so why would she want to attempt anything new?

Some of the factors that may lie behind emotional and behavioural difficulties

- Pre-natal factors – these are conditions that stem from before the child was even born, such as foetal alcohol syndrome (caused by the mother drinking too much alcohol while pregnant) or drug use in pregnancy
- Other medical conditions such as brain damage (due to lack of oxygen at birth or subsequent accident, etc)
- Learning difficulties, such as dyslexia, which can be frustrating and demoralising for the child, and attention deficit hyperactivity disorder, which means that children find it very difficult to sit quietly and listen, focus, or concentrate
- Early experiences of stress and trauma, which can have a long-term impact on her developing brain and physiology (see above)
- A previous chaotic family life with no boundaries, routines or discipline
- Previous experience of harsh or inconsistent discipline
- Growing up in a family where criminal behaviour is seen as the norm and the child is never taught, for example, that stealing is wrong
- Having poor role models, with their parents and other people around them being prone to sudden rages, which can cause children to believe that shouting, hitting people or throwing things is the normal way to behave
- Being in an environment in which they cannot be sure if adults will meet their needs – see below.

Children's unmet needs

Looked after children may have had a number of unmet needs in their early life. For example:

- Nurturing attention from adults
- Structure and everyday routines
- Excitement and stimulation
- Appropriate level of responsibility (they may have been given too much responsibility or not allowed enough)

- Support to increase their self-esteem and resilience.

Recognising the reasons that may lie behind a child's behaviour is helpful because it means you are less likely to get angry or get into a negative cycle of reacting to the child. Instead, you can try to identify the need the child is experiencing and consider different ways of responding to her.

The relationship between need and difficult behaviours

Behaviour can be a way of ensuring that our needs are met. Although it may be difficult to cope with when you are the carer, a child's undesirable behaviour is simply her attempt to have some need met. The need is valid, even if the behaviour is unacceptable.

Children who have received responsive, sensitive, consistent care from the adults in their lives will have some understanding of their needs and how to express them. These children will be aware of when they are hungry and be able to ask for something to eat or, when they are scared, seek reassurance. Children brought up in abusive and/or neglectful environments may be both less aware of what they need and less able to express their needs in acceptable ways.

These children may have developed certain behaviours as a way of keeping themselves safe or getting some sort of response to their needs in a dysfunctional household. These ways of behaving or coping mechanisms make perfect sense for a child trying to survive in those environments; but then, when they bring those behaviours with them into the foster home, the behaviours are no longer appropriate and can be seen as problematic. The behaviours are, as psychologists put it, "maladaptive".

For example, hoarding food is a way of surviving in an environment in which you can never be sure you will be given food regularly. However, in a foster home, taking food from the cupboards or fridge without asking, and hiding it under your bed where it lies uneaten and goes mouldy, can be seen as problem behaviour. That's an obvious one – but it's not always so clear what the underlying need might be. There are likely to be many other more subtle behaviours not so easily recognised as maladaptive that can arouse strong feelings of anger, hopelessness, hurt, annoyance, alarm or worry in carers. These behaviours – and the feelings they evoke – indicate that children probably need comfort, attention or reassurance.

Some children who have been brought up in a chaotic, tense, rowdy household may even try to re-create it in the foster home, because a calm, ordered environment may feel very strange to them. Some will have negative expectations of adults and will bring these into their foster families.

The ABC of behaviour: a model for understanding how behaviour is learned

Most behaviour is learned – which means it is shaped by our environment, in particular by our interactions with other people. Other people's responses can make it more or less likely that we will behave in a particular way.

For example, if you go out of your way to cook a nice meal for a friend and the friend is genuinely enthusiastic and appreciative, you will probably want to do it again another time. If, on the other hand, the friend takes your efforts for granted, you will be less inclined to bother again.

The ABC model

The ABC model provides a simple way of thinking about behaviour:

A is the antecedent or trigger which comes before the behaviour

B is the behaviour

C is the consequence, or what comes after the behaviour

Behaviour is influenced both by what comes before it – its antecedent or trigger – and by its consequences. So it may be possible to change the antecedents and the consequences in order to produce changes in behaviour.

Antecedents or triggers occur immediately before the behaviour. They might be to do with when, where and with whom the particular behaviour occurs. For example:

- A **place**, a particular **person** or **situation** can act as a trigger. For example, your child might be prone to tantrums at the supermarket checkout when she can see sweets on display; or she might be emotionally volatile when she is about to have a visit to her birth family or has just returned from seeing them; or bedtime might be the trigger time for crying or playing up.
- **Social cues** – such as criticism or even just a look or tone of voice that the child perceives as hostile – can trigger a response.
- **Copying** – children copy both appropriate and inappropriate behaviour; for instance, they may copy something they have seen someone do on television or the behaviour of other children in school.
- **Triggers from the past.** The easiest triggers to understand are those that occur in the present, but sometimes memories from the past can act as a trigger. For instance, a child who was abused at bathtime may respond with fear or aggression when her carer tells her to have a bath. The memory of the abuse evokes unpleasant thoughts and feelings, which then affect the way the child behaves. Foster carers are, of course, not always aware of children's past experiences so sometimes find it hard to understand their behaviour.
- **Self-talk.** We all have certain beliefs about ourselves and the world. A child who has negative beliefs about herself, for instance, because she has been told that she is stupid or clumsy, may try to avoid or withdraw from situations which trigger her fear of failure. Like triggers from the past, these negative beliefs are not always obvious to other people.

Other factors that play a part

There are other factors in children's lives which, while they are not immediate triggers, do affect their behaviour. For instance, poor health, medication, a poor diet, lack of sleep, uncertainty about the future and so on can all affect the way a child reacts and responds to everyday situations.

A pay-off encourages the behaviour

When we do something and the consequence is positive or rewarding, we are more likely to repeat the behaviour. The reward or "pay-off" can come in many different forms, including praise and attention.

To strengthen a particular behaviour in a child, you need to reward it consistently and reliably, for instance, by praising the child every time she tidies her bedroom or takes her dirty plate to the kitchen. Once the behaviour has become established, occasional praise will be enough to keep it up.

If the consequence is negative or unpleasant, this makes us less likely to repeat the behaviour.

Be careful not to reward inappropriate behaviour

It may seem hard to understand, but some children are so hungry for attention that they would rather have a telling-off than no attention at all.

We create problems when we unwittingly provide pay-offs for behaviour we do not want to encourage. Attention from a carer is a powerful motivator for a child, so we need to use it carefully.

One of the problems in family life is when carers fail to reward good behaviour and inadvertently reward bad behaviour. For example, if a carer leaves a child alone and ignores her whenever she plays quietly, over time this behaviour may fade away because it is not bringing the child any rewards in terms of the carer's attention. But if the carer always takes notice of her – even with a telling-off – when she fights or argues or throws things around, this gets her the attention she wants. The attention rewards the behaviour and makes her more likely to argue, fight and throw things around again in the future.

Avoiding something unpleasant is a pay-off too

Suppose a child does not want to go to school because she is trying to avoid taking a test or is being bullied, so she cries and complains of a stomach-ache. If the carer allows her to stay off school, she is rewarding the behaviour – because the pay-off is that the child gets to avoid taking the test or confronting the bullies in the playground. It is important that the child has an opportunity to talk about her concerns and worries and she will need support and encouragement to face up to whatever has happened at school.

When one thing leads to another

Problem behaviours like tantrums and destructiveness are not in fact single, isolated behaviours but are a kind of chain of behaviours that often follow a pattern. One thing leads to another, and often the explosion can spring from something quite small.

Take this example of a typical supermarket tantrum:

1. **Child sees sweets on the shelf**
2. **Asks for sweets**
3. **Picks them up and won't let go**
4. **Starts shouting**
5. **Cries**
6. **Kicks**
7. **Runs away from carer, clutching sweets**

In the early stages of this process the child may still be open to reason, firmness or distraction. But once the behaviour has escalated beyond a certain point, it's very hard to stop it. You get tense and annoyed yourself and may also start shouting. This actually makes the child's tantrum even worse. One of the following scenarios usually follows:

1. **Carer gives in and buys the sweets, in desperation or anger. Child learns that behaving badly will get her what she wants.**
2. **Furious carer grabs child and storms out of supermarket. Child gets message that to get people to do what you want, you use threats, force and intimidation.**

Of course we are all only human and scenes like this can happen in most families at times, despite our best intentions, but it's better to break the vicious circle before things get out of control on both sides.

You might not be able to stop all the tantrums, all the time – but the way you respond when trouble is brewing can certainly make a big difference to the child's behaviour.

How?

- **Be clear and consistent about your intentions – being vague, irritated or inconsistent will probably make the child behave even more badly.**
- **Keep your cool!**
- **Use distraction whenever you can – get the child to think about something else. Prevent a full-blown tantrum by distracting the child at an early stage of the process. For example, ask her to come and choose a dessert or breakfast cereal, or to choose a new toothbrush for herself.**

Removing the trigger

The two brothers Claudia was fostering were taken to school by cab. She and the boys would sit in the back. Claudia would sit Peter in the middle because he was the youngest. The boys would constantly fight in the back of the cab on the way to and from school.

Thinking about the problem, Claudia realised that one of the triggers for the fights was the boys sitting next to each other and winding each other up. So instead, she sat in the middle between them every day. Problem solved!

Claudia says: 'Some of the strategies are so simple, you think: Why didn't I think of that before?'

TRIGGERS AND PAYOFFS

Over the course of the next couple of days, explore how your child's behaviour is influenced by what happens before a particular behaviour and what happens afterwards. Try to notice the triggers for certain behaviours and the pay-offs for the child. Here are some examples:

- You ask your child to tidy her room – this is the trigger.
  Your child tidies her room. The pay-off is that you are pleased with her and give her some attention and praise.
- Your child didn't sleep well last night which means she is tired and irritable.
  You take her shopping with you and she has a tantrum because you won't buy her sweets. The trigger is the sight of the sweets in the shop. If you give in and buy them, you are providing a pay-off for the tantrum and making it more likely that it will happen again next time. If you keep your cool and refuse to buy the sweets, it will make a tantrum a little less likely next time.
- You tell the child she can watch television when she has done her homework.
  She argues and complains – which you ignore – but does her homework anyway. The pay-off is that she gets to watch television.
- Your child sees you cooking – this is the trigger – and wants to help.
  You both enjoy the time you spend together, preparing the meal. This – and the family's praise for the meal – are the pay-offs.
- Your child steals a bar of chocolate from the shop.
  She does not get caught. The pay-offs are getting chocolate for nothing and feeling smarter than adults – it makes her more likely to repeat the behaviour in future.
- She steals a bar of chocolate from the shop.
  You catch her doing it and make her give it back and apologise. As a

consequence, she is not allowed to go out and play or watch any television that evening. This makes it less likely that she will repeat the behaviour in future.

Take an objective look

For a foster carer, a child's difficult behaviour can sometimes be overwhelming. There can be a tendency to focus on how bad the behaviour makes you feel – how tiring, annoying or upsetting it is to you – rather than looking at what she is doing. You can also find yourself getting into a negative frame of mind about the child, so that you don't notice the good things about the child or the positive things she does.

Sometimes we also read things into the child's behaviour that might not be accurate – such as "she's just doing this to wind me up".

If you can take an objective look at what is happening with the child's behaviour – what exactly she is saying or doing, and how frequently – it can help you to take a step back from your own feelings about the behaviour and help you manage your emotions better. Try keeping notes or a diary, below.

Make a note of some of the behaviours you observe in your child over the next couple of days, with their triggers and pay-offs.

Remember that observing helps us to get a clearer picture and to see things in context. It also helps us to have a more objective record of what actually happens. And recording it will help you look back, reflect and see if and when things changed.

BEHAVIOUR	WHAT TRIGGERED IT?	WHAT WAS THE PAY-OFF, IF ANY?	COMMENT

BEHAVIOUR	WHAT TRIGGERED IT?	WHAT WAS THE PAY-OFF, IF ANY?	COMMENT

2 Mindfulness and caring for children

What we tell ourselves about a situation affects how we feel about it, and therefore how we behave. This chapter will look at how we can transform negative and self-defeating patterns of thought into something that helps and empowers us to deal with situations.

Caring for children can be rewarding. But at times it also inevitably evokes uncomfortable emotions of anger, sadness, frustration and anxiety, and these emotions can sometimes affect the way we respond to children. But we can learn to explore these links and manage our own feelings more effectively.

Negative self-talk

According to cognitive theory, the way we think about an event determines our emotional response. It is the way we interpret the event – the meaning we give to it – that determines how relaxed or stressed we feel about it.

The term sometimes used to refer to negative and unhelpful thoughts is "negative self-talk".

Suppose a child helps himself to food out of the fridge and eats it in the living room, making a mess on the carpet. Here are two ways the carer might respond:

- **The carer might feel angry and hostile to the child.**

  She might think: 'He is so selfish and inconsiderate! I cannot trust him for a moment!'

  In this state of mind, she is likely to criticise or shout at the child.

- **The carer might feel hopeless and demoralised.**

  She might think: 'He takes no notice of what I say. Everyone walks over me. I have no authority.'

  In this state of mind, she is likely to complain to the child but not to be assertive or follow through with any consequences.

A more constructive take on the situation would be for the carer to think about it in a way that does not bring her down:

'He knows he shouldn't take food without asking and eat it in the living room. I need to go through the house rules with him again. In the meantime, he must come and clear up after himself.'

This is a more effective and assertive coping response and leaves the carer feeling more energised and motivated to tackle the problem.

So we sometimes make a difficult situation even worse for ourselves by the way we interpret and judge it. Our thoughts affect our reaction to it.

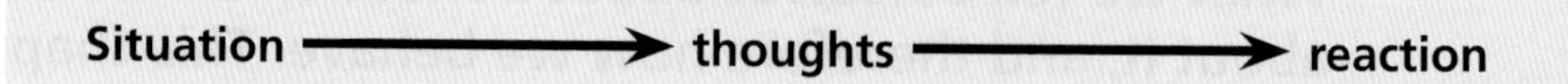

Exploring difficult feelings

Think about the following points and write down what comes to mind:

- **How do you know when you are stressed? How does your body feel? What are the physical sensations?**

- **How does stress affect the way you behave?**

- **Think of three situations that make you feel stressed**

- **Now try to tease out the negative thoughts that you tend to have in those situations. What messages do you tend to give yourself? These messages are the negative self-talk that helps trigger the sensations of stress.**

The kind of messages that make us feel bad are often things like this:

I can't cope
He's out of control
I can't manage him
Nothing I do will work with him
It's hopeless
I'm useless
My life is a mess

In other words, we tend to beat ourselves up when things aren't going well – when we do this, we are not helping ourselves!

Recognising negative thoughts

Our behaviour and feelings are both powerfully influenced by our thoughts. We recognise our feelings because we know the signs that we are stressed, sad, anxious and so on. We also know how we tend to behave when we are aware of these emotions.

In contrast, we are often less aware of our negative thoughts. Yet a negative thought can set in motion a chain of responses, so we need to recognise these thoughts.

When we have identified the negative thought or belief, we can then decide whether it is valid and replace it with a more constructive and coping thought. This takes practice.

In a nutshell, here's how it's done.

- Notice unpleasant feelings, emotional responses and/or tension in the body – for instance, feeling anxious, jittery, churning stomach, sleeplessness.
- Identify what was going through your head to make you feel this way.
- Decrease the negative thoughts using a number of different strategies – which are outlined on pages **21–24**.

Signs of negative thinking

To identify negative thoughts, we need to know what to look for. These are some of the signs:

- **Generalisations**: 'He's selfish', 'She's greedy' – labels like these tend to imply that the problem is permanent and nothing will change it.
- **Exaggeration**: often involving words like "everybody", "nobody", "always" and "never" – 'I never get anything right', 'nobody ever listens to me'.
- **Extreme expectations**: No one is perfect yet some of us think we should be. For example, you might expect yourself never to lose patience with a child or always to have a clean and tidy house, and you feel like a failure when you can't live up to your own high expectations.

- **The "shoulds" and "oughts"**: We often have ideas about how things "ought" to be and how people "should" behave, but reality falls short of our ideals. This can leave us feeling let down, cheated and angry.
- **Mind-reading**: We may find ourselves making assumptions about other people's thoughts and feelings. 'I can't say no to him because he will blow his top'; 'she didn't phone me because she doesn't care about me.' These beliefs affect what we do and how we react – but the trouble is that our beliefs may be quite wrong.
- **Turning things into a catastrophe**: This is what we do when we think: 'That's the last straw' or 'I can't cope with another thing going wrong.' By telling yourself the situation is disastrous, you are making yourself feel desperate and powerless.

Negative thoughts make us feel more emotional – which impairs our ability to think and act rationally.

Decreasing negative thoughts

What we need to do is examine, challenge and reject our inaccurate negative thoughts. Then we need to replace them with thoughts that are more positive, constructive and helpful to us. Here are some examples:

- **Replace generalisations** with thoughts that are more specific and acknowledge the positives as well as the negatives. See below for some examples and see if you can add an example of your own:

Generalisation
He's completely selfish and irresponsible.

More accurate thought
He can be self-absorbed, but at other times he is very thoughtful and kind.

Generalisation
I'm an insensitive person.

More accurate thought
Sometimes I make insensitive comments but most of the time I am understanding and caring.

Generalisation
Nobody ever listens to me.

More accurate thought
The children have not been co-operative today, but yesterday they were good and I will be more assertive with them tomorrow.

- **Keep things in perspective**. In most situations you can remind yourself that, in your shoes, many other people would be feeling the same as you. Here are some examples – see if you can add another example of your own.

Seeing problems as extreme	Seeing problems as normal
When she screams at me I just can't stand it – I feel as though I'm going mad.	I feel all wound up and upset when she screams at me, but that's natural.
Today was the worst day ever and if things don't improve, I can't go on.	Everyone has bad days sometimes.
No other child would talk to me like that.	He is sometimes defiant, like lots of other looked after children.

- **Substitute more positive and coping thoughts.** When your thoughts are negative and bringing you down, try repeating something more calming and positive that will help you cope. Here are a couple of examples. Can you think of another?

Negative thought	Positive thought
Things can't get any worse.	This is difficult but it's not the end of the world. I can deal with it.
This child is totally disorganised and can't concentrate – she'll never do well at school.	She needs my support and encouragement to help her learn to focus and concentrate.

- **Dispute absolutes.** Stop striving for perfection, because you'll never reach it. Be more flexible and relaxed. Here are a couple of examples. Can you think of another?

Rigid expectations	Flexible expectations
I should cook a hot meal for the family every evening.	Who says it's always my job to cook? I'll let someone else take a turn – or make it easy on myself by getting a ready meal sometimes.
Ayesha should do as she is told, every time.	What makes me think she must be 100 per cent obedient? No child could manage that.

- **Don't try to mind-read.** If you assume you know about other people's intentions, you could get it wrong and get angry or upset for nothing. Instead, focus on the behaviour you want to change. This will leave you feeling more positive and in control. For example:

Mind-reading	Focus on behaviour
Jasmin has deliberately left her clothes on the floor because she knows it winds me up.	**Jasmin has a problem with putting her clothes away. I'll talk to her about setting up a reward chart to encourage her to pick them up and put them away.**
Robert chews with his mouth open because he knows we all hate it.	**Robert needs to develop better table manners – how can we help him?**

- **Be objective about situations.** Some people are prone to self-criticism and tend to blame themselves or take it personally when things go wrong. This just makes you feel depressed and ineffectual. It's more constructive if you can step back and look at things less personally. For example:

Blaming yourself	Being objective
I'm a soft touch – I'm useless at getting Lauren to do anything for herself.	**What would I like Lauren to do? How can I help her with this? What can I do differently?**
Robbie accidentally broke our train set and now everyone is upset – it's my fault, I shouldn't have let him play with it.	**I decided to give him the chance to play with it but it didn't work out the way I planned. Still, I can't watch him every minute. The children will have to accept that toys do sometimes break. We can replace the broken train.**

- **Acknowledge your own strengths and abilities.** Most of us have a tendency to criticise ourselves far more than we praise ourselves! We need to learn to value our efforts and achievements and give ourselves a pat on the back sometimes. If you get into the habit of being kinder to yourself, your confidence and self-esteem will grow.

  You can be a good role model for the child if you show him that it's OK to be positive about yourself and your achievements. Here are some examples. Can you think of any others?

You can say nothing...	Or you can model self-praise and positive thinking
	I didn't overreact when our neighbour came to complain about your behaviour. I listened to him and was assertive and took action. I'm very pleased with myself.
	I think I organised your birthday party very well – everyone enjoyed the games and I was proud of the birthday cake I made for you.

- **Use humour.** Laughter dispels any tension and helps us deal with situations more calmly. So try to avoid the tendency to take things too seriously. For example:

Taking things too seriously	Using humour
Your bedroom is a tip and it's a disgrace to the family. You have got to clear it up or it's going to become a serious health hazard.	Look at your room – for a minute, I thought we'd had burglars! Better take your dirty plates downstairs to the kitchen – or you might find little mice deciding to move in!
You haven't brushed your hair today. It's a mess. Go back to your bedroom and brush it. I don't want to be seen out with you like that.	Here's your hairbrush. Why don't you make yourself look beautiful before we go out?
The kids have all been squabbling and screaming all day. I can't stand this! It's just impossible!	The kids have been horrible today. They've excelled themselves. I think it's a plot to drive me mad. But they'll never win!

Use coping statements

We have seen how you can challenge your own negative thoughts and replace them with more constructive thoughts.

Something else you can do is to use affirmations or "coping statements" to give yourself encouragement when things are tough. This is a form of "positive self-talk" that can help to keep you calm and give you courage to face difficult situations.

Coping statements should be short, start with "I..." and be in the present tense. Here are some examples:

Coping statements

I can get through this. I will cope.
I'm a good carer. He needs me to keep calm and remain firm.
I've done this before and I know it's going to be OK.
I need to just breathe slowly and stay calm.
I can do it. It will work.

Think about some stressful situations you could have to face. Think about the kind of statements that would help to counteract the negative messages that might be in your head.

Write down your own personal coping statements below. The wording should make you feel good. It should be relevant and achievable.

Potential stressful situation	Personal coping statement
______________________	______________________
______________________	______________________
______________________	______________________
______________________	______________________
______________________	______________________
______________________	______________________
______________________	______________________
______________________	______________________

Developing a more positive thinking style can reduce our levels of stress and allow us to act more constructively and effectively.

Using these ideas to help your child

Once you discover what a difference this can make, you can use it with your child too.

- Set an example yourself with the things you say.
- Let him see you responding calmly to difficult situations and people.
- Encourage him to think more positively and constructively about himself and other people.
- When he is expressing negative thoughts, challenge them – present him with a more accurate, positive thought.

Helping children to talk about feelings

Sally was fostering six-year-old twins who had suffered emotional abuse.

'For a long time Rosie was an "angel" – so well-behaved that when I told people about her, they would say "there's no such child". But after a few months the tears started. She would be crying every two minutes and saying things about herself like "I hate myself, I'm not a nice person, I wish I was dead".

'Whenever they had had contact with their birth parents, their behaviour was always particularly challenging. When Rosie is upset I ask her to tell me about it. If I don't push too much and let her take it at her own pace, she will eventually come out with it and say: "What if they take me away from you?"

'I teach the children that they are safe with me and that they can come to me if there's anything they want to talk about.'

The importance of modelling

One of the ways children learn is by observing others. They observe how the other children and adults around them behave and they see the consequences of the behaviour (e.g. if another child does something "naughty" and is told off, the child may learn from observing this that the particular action is not a good idea). They may imitate both appropriate and inappropriate behaviour they have seen. So one of the ways adults can help children learn appropriate behaviour is by "modelling" it in front of them. If an adult consistently demonstrates certain behaviours – such as responding cheerfully and calmly when something goes wrong rather than losing their temper or treating it like a catastrophe – then this shows the child the appropriate way to respond.

Using these ideas to help your child

Once you discover what a difference positive thinking can make, you can use it with your child too.

- Set an example yourself with the things you say.
- Be a good role model! Let him see you responding calmly to difficult situations and people.

- Encourage him to think more positively and constructively about himself and other people.
- When he is expressing negative thoughts, challenge them – present him with a more accurate, positive thought.

The "mindfulness" approach

For most parents and carers, life is busy and there are many demands on our time, which means we are often on "automatic pilot" and it can be hard to focus on the here and now. In caring for children, we need to stay in the present moment to sense what might be required. What worked yesterday isn't necessarily going to work today.

Looking after children is a complex and often stressful task. When our own inner resources are depleted, we have to have effective and healthy ways to replenish them and to restore ourselves.

Practising "mindfulness" can help with both of these things. Mindfulness is the practice of living in the present moment and is a powerful way of paying closer attention to the things that are truly important. It can help with stress by helping us to tolerate a feeling and circumstance that cannot be changed right now. It can help us to remain calm until it is an appropriate time to find a solution. It allows us to "sit with" the difficult feeling until we can manage the situation. Research has shown that regular mindfulness practice can help more generally with managing stress; and it's also shown that "mindfulness" can be helpful in parenting by reducing parental stress and reactivity and reducing parents' preoccupation with children's problems.

The more you practise mindfulness, the more you will be able to develop the quality of being present, available and sensitive to your child during your day-to-day life together. You might also find it helps with your general stress levels and your ability to concentrate and to cope with the demands and challenges facing you.

Originating in Buddhist meditation, the practice of mindfulness is now making its way into the mainstream of western society in many different contexts.

To become "mindful" means to cultivate the ability to pay conscious attention to whatever you are doing in each moment. It's about being fully "present" in every situation. Here's a simple example: when you are playing a game with your child in a "mindful" way, you are fully focused on the game – your mind is not wandering, planning the evening's meal or noting the dust on the mantelpiece and wondering when you are going to get time to clean. The quality of your relationships, moment-to-moment, is important – it is expressed in how you say good morning, how you pass the milk at the breakfast table, how you notice something good that your child is doing and praise it, rather than in the special occasions or the once-a-year holiday.

Mindfulness is also about noticing any associations and judgements that you have. It is about noticing these and then letting go of them, if only for that moment.

Mindfulness is a skill that takes practice and commitment. It is not easy at first as our brains are used to being busy and managing many demands at once. It is best to start practising mindfulness when you are feeling calm and relaxed – just as, when you are learning to swim, it is best to practise in the shallow end first rather than waiting until you are drowning before trying to learn.

One way of getting started is to become aware of your breath as it moves in and out. Doing this regularly – ideally, once or twice a day – could gradually affect the way you feel at other times too. If you would like to explore and develop mindfulness further, there are many books, apps and courses around.

The following quotation helps explain how to use your breath in practising mindfulness. Your breath brings you back to the here and now.

Use the breath as an anchor to tether your attention to the present moment. Your thinking mind will drift here and there, depending on the currents and winds moving in the mind until, at some point, the anchor line grows taut and brings you back

Kabat-Zinn, 2004

Below is an exercise that will help you to focus on the present moment and practise being fully present in the situation you are in. You could use this whenever you feel the need.

Mindfulness breathing exercise

This mindfulness exercise involves pausing, watching our breath, and noticing when our attention leaves our breath (for example, because we get lost in thoughts, distracted by a sensation inside or outside ourselves, or caught up in an emotion).

- First, sit comfortably. Place your feet shoulder-width apart, flat on the ground. Make sure you are physically comfortable.
- Now close your eyes and gently focus your attention on your breathing. Breathe in through your nose and out through your mouth. Breathe so that the air enters your diaphragm – just at the bottom of your ribcage. Notice your abdomen rising and falling as you breathe in and out.
- Try to stay focused on your breath.
- Notice when your attention drifts off away from your breath. When you notice that your attention has left your breath, just gently bring it back to your breath, again and again, over and over. It is very normal and natural for our attention to wander. The purpose of this exercise is to practise bringing our attention back to our breath.
- You may find it helpful to focus on how the air feels as it enters your nose and how it feels slightly warmer as it leaves your mouth.
- You may like to place your hands on your stomach to focus your attention on the rise and fall of your abdomen.
- Just keep breathing and focusing your attention on your breath.
- After around five minutes, or when you're ready, gently open your eyes.

3 Praise to promote positive behaviour

Most children respond well to praise, encouragement and positive attention.

In many children, these alone are enough to help them behave well. They are the foundation of a warm, positive relationship with carers. Without this kind of relationship, it is hard to exert any kind of discipline.

In this and the following two chapters, we will be looking at some of the main things you can use to encourage positive skills and behaviours in a child: praise, positive attention and tangible rewards.

Focus on the positive

Some children are so difficult that it's all too easy to get preoccupied with their problem behaviour. If you can't improve the way they behave, you can become demoralised and feel that you spend all your time nagging them or telling them off. The child feels that she can't do anything right and the atmosphere at home becomes increasingly negative and tense. You end up having to punish her frequently for bad behaviour and things get even worse.

The trick is to break this negative cycle. You need to start to focus on the positive things the child does – however few and far between – and provide praise and encouragement for those. Many looked after children have experienced nothing but negative responses. If you can start to look out for the child's positive actions and qualities, it will help you as well as her. You will stop focusing on the problems and both you and the child will start to feel better. Your warmth, praise and positive attitude will make for a better relationship between you. Because of this relationship, the child will want to behave well to please you.

REWARDING WITH PRAISE

Praise is an important way of providing a reward for positive behaviour. It shows the child that you have noticed she is behaving well.

Praise can be a smile, a pat on the back or a thumbs-up as well as words.

When children are playing quietly or getting on with what they are meant to be doing, often carers don't think to praise them. However, if good behaviour goes unnoticed, the child may be more likely to start misbehaving in order to get attention.

- Use praise to provide positive attention for behaviour you want to encourage.
- Avoid giving any attention to minor inappropriate behaviour, where possible; in other words, ignore behaviour you want to discourage. This applies particularly to behaviour that is aimed at gaining your negative attention.

She never does anything I can praise her for!

Some children's behaviour is so poor that it can be hard to find anything to be pleased about. With these children, you have to make a conscious effort to "catch them being good" so you can give them some praise. Or you can set up situations or make requests that you are reasonably sure they will comply with – like 'please could you bring in the biscuits from the kitchen?' That way, the child can have the experience of being co-operative and pleasing you and being praised for this.

You can also praise children for not doing the things they usually do – for instance, 'Kirsty, you've had no fights tonight. I've really enjoyed being with you and your brothers. Well done!'

How do you feel about praise?

Think back to your own childhood, to a particular occasion when you were praised either at home or at school, or a time when you wanted to be praised but were not. Think about how this experience made you feel. Did it change your behaviour? Did the praise spur you on, or did the lack of praise discourage you from trying again? Did the praise change the way you thought or felt about yourself?

How do you feel now when someone says something nice about you or compliments you? Some people find it hard to accept compliments.

Reflecting on your own experience could help you gain a deeper understanding of the effect of praise on the child you are looking after.

Sometimes, our own feelings and attitudes can get in the way of our being good at giving praise to children. Our own childhood experiences of being praised – or not – can affect the way we feel about giving praise. For instance:

- Some people feel unnatural or awkward giving praise.
- Some believe we should praise children only for exceptionally good behaviour or achievements.
- Some believe that praise will somehow spoil the child or go to their head.

Praise can be surprisingly powerful in motivating a child. It helps them to feel more positive about themselves and encourages good behaviour.

Praising doesn't come easily to everyone and we need to practise.

Think about how you use praise with the children you look after. Are you sparing with your praise or do you provide lots of warm, enthusiastic, positive messages?

Some children find praise hard to take. They may have a very negative image of themselves and cannot accept warmth and encouragement.

Sometimes carers feel unappreciated and don't get the praise they deserve. To practise your skills in praising, start by praising yourself. Here are some positive thoughts to get you started. Finish the sentences we have started.

Now add two more positive thoughts about yourself. You can do it!

Praise yourself!

I am a good carer because ______________________

My best qualities are ______________________

I am proud of the way I ______________________

I have helped my child by ______________________

____

____

Remember, carers need to value themselves if they are to be positive role models for the children in their care. So don't be afraid of praising yourself!

Self-praise is a valuable skill for children to develop – it can help them feel more positive about themselves. By praising yourself out loud in front of her, you are showing her how it's done.

PRAISING: HOW TO MAKE THE MOST OF IT

You can use praise as a reward to encourage behaviour you would like to see more of. For instance, if you know that your child tends to be quite rough when playing with younger children, you can make a point of praising her whenever she plays nicely with them.

Praise works best when it is:

- **Specific, rather than vague or general.** If you say 'Good girl!' or 'Well done!', the child may not be clear about what it is they have actually done. Effective praise spells it out: 'I'm really pleased you are trying so hard to work through your maths homework', or 'Thank you for doing as I asked straight away'. This extra information helps looked after children to learn what is expected of them.
- **Sincere.** Praise delivered without any enthusiasm or eye contact is not as rewarding. So think about all the non-verbal aspects of your praise: the way you stop what you are doing and:
  - make eye contact;
  - the warmth and energy in your voice;
  - your touch; and
  - your smile.

  Even if this doesn't feel very natural to you at first, you can practise it and learn to express yourself in this way.
- **Immediate.** Praise works best when it comes straight after the positive behaviour. That way, the child can make the link between the behaviour and the reward. If you are trying to encourage a behaviour that doesn't happen very often, you need to look out for it and give lots of praise as soon as you notice the child doing it. It is important to praise the child as soon as she starts doing something – such as tidying away her toys – rather than waiting until she has finished and everything is put away. Praising her while she is tidying is encouraging for her and shows her that you have noticed and are pleased.
- **Appropriate.** Don't praise a child for playing with her little sister if, in fact, she is pulling faces and teasing her. Children need to be clear about what behaviour you want to see.

What to praise?

Here are some of the behaviours some carers have chosen to praise:

- Playing co-operatively with other children
- Eating a meal without messing around
- Speaking in a calm voice rather than shouting
- Saying please and thank you
- Doing as she is told the first time
- Being kind to the family pet
- Trying hard with a difficult task
- Trying again when something didn't work the first time
- Saying something nice to someone

School work might have become a source of anxiety and failure for the child, so look out for any small successes for which you can give her praise. Focus on what she is doing well rather than her mistakes.

Praise for doing and praise for being

Praise for **doing** looks at a child's cognitive, social and behavioural skills. These may include things like listening well, thinking hard and taking turns. The more you are able to praise these skills, the more likely it is that a child will recognise what kind of behaviour you want to see.

Praise for **being** is about valuing children for who they are and their personal qualities – such as thoughtfulness, enthusiasm, being kind and caring. It's all too easy to focus praise on **what children do** rather than **who they are** – but it's essential that children also receive positive messages about who they are to help them feel good about themselves, which adds to their personal strength and resilience as they go through life.

Praise to support learning

Use praise to support your child's learning skills as well as her behaviour: skills such as co-operating with others, listening, concentrating, following instructions and sitting still can all help your child have a positive school experience. Praising these behaviours at home gives the child positive feedback and helps her develop the foundation skills that are so important in the classroom.

Why reading matters so much

Reading is an important life skill, and carers can do a lot to ensure that reading is a regular and rewarding activity for the children they care for.

Reading with children can help to promote the attachment between you and the child. It can provide a safe and intimate space in which the child can not only learn to read more fluently but also learn about and discuss the world. Reading introduces a child to a range of ideas and stories that will be helpful in developing her understanding of the world. Being a good reader can increase confidence and self-esteem, helping to foster greater resilience.

When children are wary of learning or scared of getting things wrong, homework can become something to be feared or avoided, and can turn into a battleground. To help your child get to grips with homework, avoid criticism and tension, praise any effort frequently, and ignore minor misbehaviour. Praising her can help make homework a more positive experience for both of you.

Tips on encouraging children to read

With some children you may have to work quite hard at first to engage them in reading. Here are some tips:

- Make sure you give your undivided attention
- Read with your child for at least 10 minutes a day
- Sit next to your child
- Be warm and loving
- Be positive and encourage your child's interest
- Praise your child for how well she is doing
- Tell your child you are enjoying spending this time with her
- Try to find books and other things to read that tap into your child's interests; whatever they want to read is OK, even if they prefer comics
- Reward reluctant readers
- Have fun

Avoid diluting praise with criticism

Praise should never be combined with a "put-down" – such as 'Well done for finishing your homework, but you really could have done it more neatly' or 'I'm pleased you've tidied your room – what a shame it took you three days to do it'. This spoils the effect of the praise and can be demotivating for the child, who may hold on to the negative message.

Praise small steps

If you want your child to learn how to dress herself, you might need to start by praising every little thing she does, like picking up a sock and putting it half-on her foot. Praise her for these small steps and it will encourage her to try out more.

Praise her for trying

If your child tries to do something you want her to do, praise her for her efforts even if she doesn't quite manage it.

Spontaneous praise and targeted praise

Spontaneous praise is the kind of praise you give, at any time, for good behaviour. Targeted praise is used when you have identified a problem behaviour, and you then praise the child for the opposite and desired behaviour ("target behaviour"), whenever it occurs. So, you could think of a behaviour that you want to see instead of a problem behaviour, for example, talking quietly or politely instead of shouting, and then praising the appropriate behaviour whenever it occurs.

Use praise to "shape" behaviour

You can use praise to help children develop and establish behaviours that they are not yet very good at or that they are struggling with. In psychology, a technique called "shaping" is used to bring about a desired behaviour that is very unlikely to happen by itself. Shaping is used when you can't wait for the desired behaviour to happen in order to praise it, because it's highly unlikely that it will occur out of the blue, without adult help but instead you reinforce behaviours that get progressively closer to the particular behaviour you want to see.

This is how it works. Each time the child masters a particular stage, you praise her; but over time, she needs to get a little bit closer to the desired behaviour to earn the praise. This way, you encourage her to gradually learn the steps involved in the new behaviour or skill – eventually she will master the desired behaviour and then, of course, you can give lots of praise.

For example, suppose the target behaviour is for the child to clean out her hamster's cage by herself. At first you could praise her just for getting together all the cleaning materials and other things that are needed to clean out the cage, and for watching while you do it. Then, once she's reliably doing that, you could praise her for putting the new wood shavings and bedding and fresh food into the cage once you've cleaned it out. Eventually, one day she will do the whole job by herself – and you can give her lots of praise for doing it!

On one of those bad days when your child is playing up and you both feel irritable, try to find something, anything, to praise her for. You might just find saying something positive breaks the negative cycle, changes the mood and leaves you both feeling better.

SHAPING BEHAVIOUR

Is there a task or behaviour you would like your child to be able to do, that she can't manage at the moment? Perhaps you'd like to encourage a timid older child to be able to go to the corner shop on his own and buy something. Perhaps you'd like a child to be able to get dressed all by herself or to pack her schoolbag every evening with everything she will need for the next day. Think about how you could break down the task into stages that are closer and closer to what you'd like your child to do. Think about how you could praise or reward her for each of these stages to encourage her to master it.

Make a note of how long it takes the child to master each stage on the way to the desired task, and how she responds to the praise or reward.

Desired task or behaviour	How long it took	Result
Stage 1		
Stage 2		
Stage 3		

Encourage the child to praise herself

One expert (in Daniel and Wassell, 2002) has a simple model that highlights beautifully how children can identify and acknowledge resilience factors in themselves.

He says if children are able to say 'I have…', 'I am…', and 'I can…' and complete these sentences in positive and constructive ways (for example, 'I have a good friend, I am kind and I can swim'), they are acknowledging strengths that show they have a secure base, good self-esteem and self-efficacy, respectively.

Foster carers can help children to strengthen these qualities by providing a nurturing home with warm and firm boundaries (secure base); by helping children to label their skills (self-efficacy); and by encouraging them to think about and describe themselves in positive and affirming ways, emphasising their qualities and strengths (self-esteem) (Fostering Network, 2014, p 120).

Finally, remember you

Start the habit of praising yourself at least once a day for something you have done well or are pleased about. At first you might do this in your head. Then you could voice it out loud, in front of the child. This might feel a bit odd at first. Remember, you are an important role model for the child – and valuing yourself and being positive about yourself are good skills to model.

Here are a few suggestions, but you should praise yourself for whatever you are most proud of!

- I am a kind and thoughtful carer
- I am resourceful and energetic in the way I care for children
- I am open to learning and to changing
- I encourage and affirm my children
- I am a positive and cheerful person
- I am able to manage challenges
- I keep calm under extreme provocation

PRACTISE YOUR PRAISING SKILLS

Over the next couple of days, look for any opportunity to praise your child when you notice her behaving well. If it helps, jot down some ideas below. Remember to praise your child by simply describing the behaviour that you like. Here's a sample praise chart.

Day	Spontaneous praise 5x day	Targeted praise	Observations: what I said, what happened
Mon	✓✓	✓✓	Anna offered some sweets to Ben. Told her she was a kind girl to share. Praised her for saying goodnight to Ben.
Tues	✓✓	✓✓	Difficult day – Anna in trouble at school. I was cross and disappointed – found it hard to praise. Anna was sullen.
Weds	✓✓✓ ✓✓ ✓✓	✓✓✓	I tried hard to look for positives today. Anna responded well. Played for over an hour without fighting.

THERE'S NO LIMIT TO THE WAYS YOU CAN PRAISE

Some things I could praise my child for:

A good way to give praise is to tell the child how the behaviour makes you feel. Try jotting some specific things down.

I like it when you ____________________

It helps me when you ____________________

I'm so pleased that you ____________________

You've done a great job of ____________________

It is good to be descriptive in your praise. For example, 'You have used lots of beautiful bright colours in your painting' shows you have really bothered to notice what the child has done. This will mean more to the child than a more general comment like 'Fantastic picture!'

You could also praise the child indirectly by telling other people – in her presence – how good she is or how well he shas done something.

Be generous with your praise!

'It worked with us'

Claudia fostered two brothers aged eight and six. She attended the Fostering Changes *course to help her manage their challenging behaviour.*

'I had always used praise but I learned I had to use a lot more. I learned creative ways of praising rather than just always saying "Well done". It helped them feel good about what they had done and I found it was less draining for me.

'Life is so hectic and busy when you are fostering that you don't have time to think. Sometimes you get caught up in noticing the unwanted behaviours and a lot of the good behaviour passes you by. There are lots of little things you don't always have time to notice. There were sometimes quite subtle things the younger boy was doing, like being kind to someone else and sharing things, and with all the day-to-day challenges I didn't always pick up on good behaviour like this. But once I started to praise these things, I could see his whole body language change and his pleasure was obvious.'

4 Using play to build positive attention and secure relationships

What do children need to thrive? Children need adults who respond sensitively to their needs, adults with whom they can form relationships that give them the security and confidence to explore their world. For most children, these relationships begin in the early days and months of life.

A sensitive parent or carer responds to the baby's crying by soothing him and giving him what he needs. When a baby has responsive caregivers – parents or carers who pick him up and comfort him when he cries, and feed him when he is hungry – he learns that if he becomes distressed his parent or carer will come and that the world is a safe and predictable place. This becomes the basis of the baby's **secure attachment** to the caregiver(s).

Attachment

The term "attachment" is used to describe the quality of the child's relationship with their caregiver over the first few years of life. The attachment reflects the way the child and caregiver have interacted together.

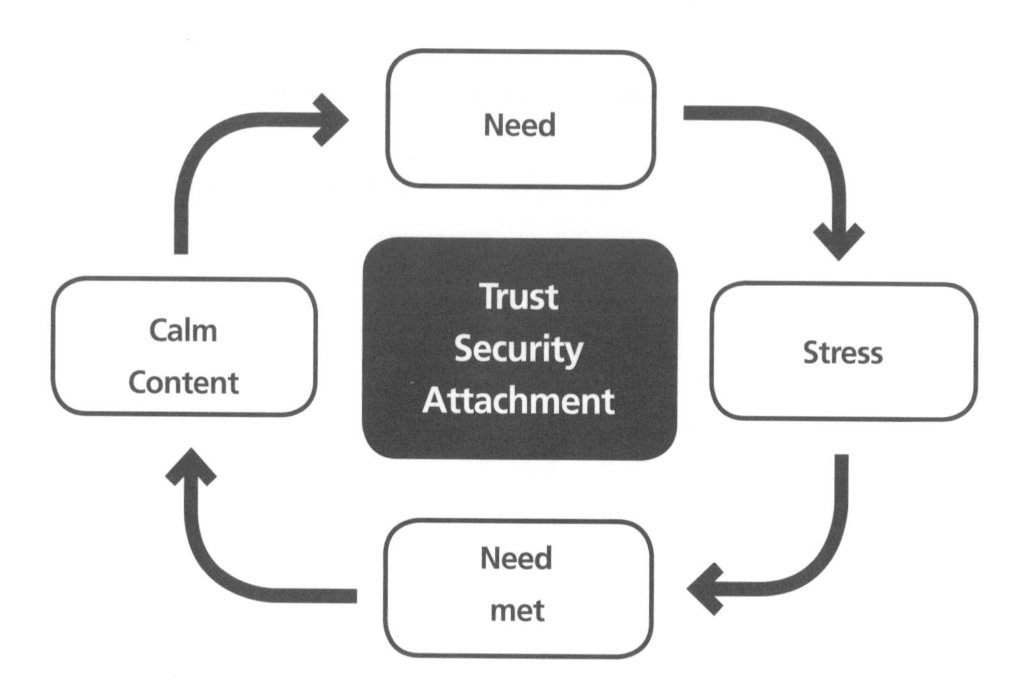

A **secure attachment** allows the child to develop the ability to regulate his emotions; in other words, to manage his arousal (anxiety and stress) and distress without becoming overwhelmed. Children with a secure attachment can use their parent or carer as a "secure base" from which to venture out and learn about the world with confidence.

Not all children develop a secure pattern of attachment. A famous research study (the Strange Situation Procedure, conducted by a psychologist called Ainsworth in 1978) looked at how infants responded when their caregiver left the room, and then subsequently returned. They categorised the infants according to the way they responded to this stress. **Securely attached** infants want comfort from the carer when she returns but are readily comforted and quickly return to play and exploring. Infants with an **insecure attachment pattern** show relatively little obvious need for comfort when the carer returns – they have learned to avoid seeking comfort and they do without it, even though they are feeling distress. This is thought to be a response to a form of caregiver interaction characterised by intrusive or insensitive responding. Another form of insecure attachment sees babies who become very distressed and seek comfort but who do not calm down when it is offered, or who mix attempts to get close with angry resistance. This is thought to result from an inconsistent or uninvolved caregiver.

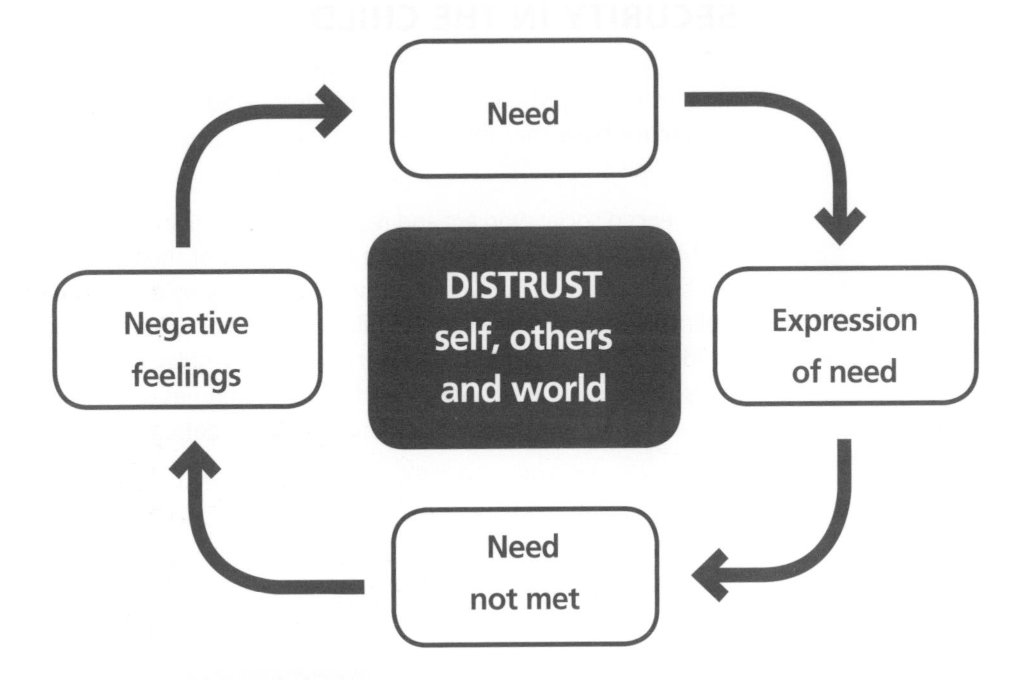

There is a third type of insecure attachment pattern that is much rarer in the general population – it is found more often in cases where children have been maltreated. This is the **insecure-disorganised** attachment pattern, where infants do not show a coherent response to the stress on their attachment system but, instead, may rock back and forth or freeze or show other odd behaviour. It is thought to be due to the experience of the caregiver being either frightening or frightened (e.g. either abusive or themselves a victim of abuse).

Many of the children who need foster care have not had their needs met as babies, thereby affecting their ability to form secure attachments. This will affect their physiological arousal levels and the way they behave when they are upset and distressed. Sometimes children have formed attachments but these have been disrupted by moves to foster care (sometimes multiple moves). This may affect the way that children will behave with you, appearing to resist or not need your comfort. This can be upsetting for carers and at times feel difficult. Remember to try and not take this personally but understand that this is a legacy of their previous relationships.

However, some children who were insecurely attached as babies and who experience a significant improvement in their lives, for example, being moved to a stable and caring foster placement, can develop a near-normal attachment to their foster carer later on.

HOW FOSTER CARERS CAN HELP BUILD TRUST AND SECURITY IN THE CHILD

As a foster carer, you can provide sensitive caregiving that will gradually help build the **secure base** that the child's own parents have been unable to provide. How do you do this?

Experienced social workers and researchers Dr Gillian Schofield and Mary Beek (2014) have developed the **secure base** model of therapeutic caregiving, which looks at the interactions of daily family life as a way of helping children develop a feeling of security. Dr Gillian Schofield is Co-Director of the Centre for Research on Children and Families at the University of East Anglia. Mary Beek has more than 20 years' experience in adoption and fostering, and has a special interest in training and supporting foster carers and adopters of older children.

Schofield and Beek's model is rooted in attachment theory. They reason that the ordinary routines of caring, nurturing, feeding, playing and communicating provide countless opportunities for caregivers to change the way children think and feel about themselves and others, thus building their trust and increasing their sense of security. The diagram below shows some of the ways foster carers can do this.

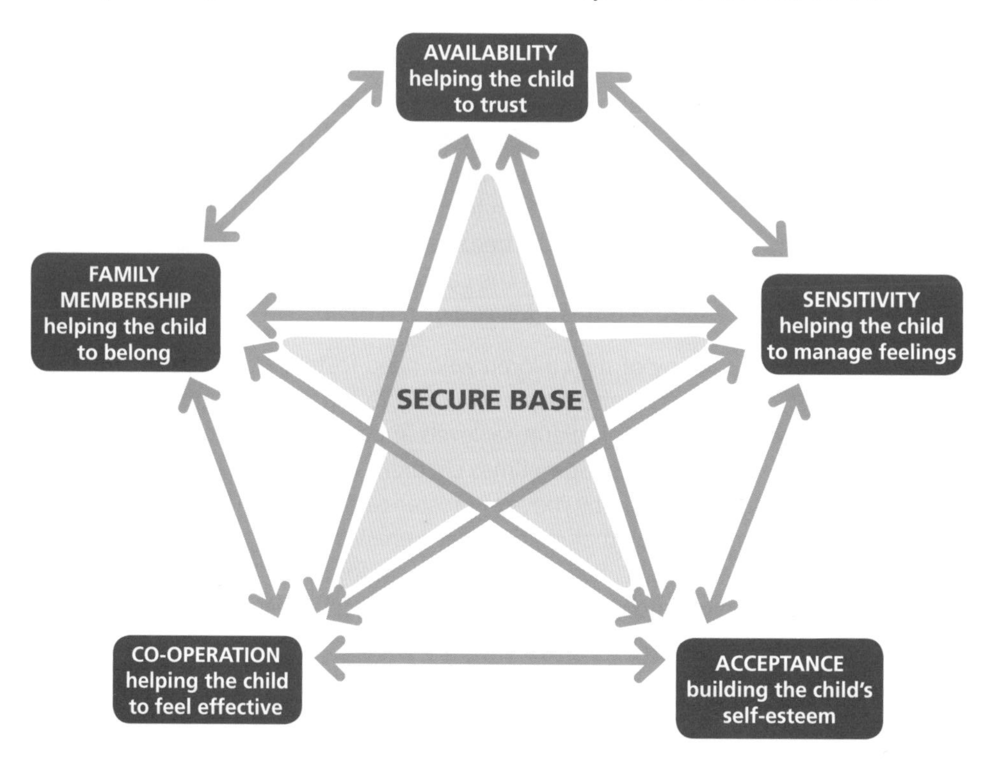

Games and activities that help build trust

Try some of these games and activities (Schofield and Beek, 2006, p. 56) with your child:

- Hand-holding games such as ring a ring o'roses
- Clapping games

- Reading stories with the child on your lap or sitting close
- Leading each other blindfolded
- Face-painting
- Three-legged race
- Throwing a ball or beanbag to each other
- Bat and ball
- Blowing and chasing bubbles together
- Rocking, singing, gently holding the child
- Rubbing lotion on to each other's hands and arms
- Brushing and plaiting hair
- Painting nails
- Teaching a new skill or learning one together

Using play to give positive attention

Many looked after children have learned, early on in their young lives, that the only way they will get any attention is by behaving badly. In their experience, they are ignored when they are quiet but they get attention – even if it's someone shouting at them – when they misbehave. Surprising as it may seem, children would rather have negative attention than none at all.

Many looked after children have not had the same opportunities to play as other children. Some need to be encouraged to play, and attending will do this.

When a child comes to you, your task is to establish the opposite pattern. You need to make sure that you target your positive attention on him when he is behaving well, and pay him as little attention as possible when he is behaving inappropriately.

Most children love it when adults are interested in them and what they are doing. One of the skills that you need to develop as a carer is to actively take notice of the child when he is being good. Paying attention to him at these times will encourage and reward him for behaving well.

This chapter explains a strategy called "attending", which is a non-threatening way of getting alongside a child and positively supporting him while he is playing. It is a way of relating to a child that involves noticing what he is doing and showing interest. At its heart, attending is about sensitive responding and is a key practical and active way of increasing trust and secure attachment between parents, carers and children. You don't try to show or tell him what to do or ask questions – you simply follow his lead.

"Attending" can be a powerful tool, especially for children who are not used to getting much positive attention from adults. If you can do it regularly, you and the child will probably start to feel much closer. It builds up trust between you and the child, and encourages him to feel more positive about himself. You may even find that his concentration improves and he can spend more time playing, even when you are not with him.

Giving the child regular positive attention in this way will also demonstrate to him that you are interested in him and that you like to spend time with him. It can send him a powerful message about his value and importance and can build a positive attachment between you.

Just 10 minutes a day can make a big difference.

How to "attend"

The good news is that, for "attending", you only need to set aside 10 minutes a day... but that 10 minutes is a special time during which you have to give your full attention to the child.

This is what you do!

- **Follow the child's lead.** Follow his ideas and imagination rather than suggesting your own. That way, he will get more absorbed in the game and it helps him come up with more ideas. If he wants you to put all the cows in the sandpit, don't question his logic – just do it!
- **Imitate what she does.** For instance, if she pushes a car along the floor, you might do the same. Mirror her actions without dominating. Use "descriptive commenting", e.g. describe what the child is doing, thus helping him be focused.
- **Go at the child's pace.** Children often like to repeat activities until they feel they have entirely mastered them. This might seem boring to adults. But resist the temptation to speed things up by introducing new ideas and activities – that could just put him under pressure to "perform".
- **Be sensitive to the child.** Play does not need to have an aim or a goal – let the child do what she wants to do and wait for her to move on to another activity when she feels like it.
- **Avoid power struggles.** Play is one area where children can find out what it feels like to exercise power and control. This can help develop their sense of competence and independence. So be careful not to do anything that might undermine him – if you are building towers, don't build one that is better than his! Remember, you want him to experience success.
- **Encourage her creativity.** It is the process of playing and experimenting that matters, not the finished product. So try not to suggest ways she could improve her picture, model or game, even if you can see how much better it could be! Praise her for her inventiveness, persistence and concentration.
- **Encourage imaginative play.** Pretending, dressing up and acting out stories with dolls or toy animals develops children's imagination. This kind of play helps them to experiment with different roles and think about other people's feelings. Imaginative play is a good opportunity for you to "attend" and enter into the fantasy world your child is creating.
- **Be an appreciative audience.** Keep focusing on the child – don't get so absorbed in your own play activity that you forget to enjoy what he is doing.
- **Laugh and have fun together!**

When an adult "attends", a child feels special. Most children love the times when their carer is attending.

What to watch out for

Remember, while you are attending, resist the temptation to:

- ask questions
- take charge
- give instructions
- teach the child.

THE RIGHT KIND OF PLAY

When you have set aside time for attending, suggest three or four suitable toys, games or activities that lend themselves to creativity and imagination and let your child choose one. Alternatively, look out for a time when he is playing with something suitable – then drop everything for ten minutes so you can give him some positive attention.

Board games are not ideal for attending, because they are competitive and highly structured. It's also hard to attend while your child plays computer games so try to avoid these too. Also to be avoided are jigsaw puzzles and any other games where there is a right and a wrong way to do something. It would be best if your child is playing with bricks, cars, dolls, Lego, crayons or paints, etc.

Descriptive commenting

Many of us are used to asking lots of questions when we play with children: 'What's that you are drawing?'; 'Do you know what colour pigs are?' Although the aim is to help the child to learn, questions can be distracting. They interrupt the child's play and introduce the adult's agenda.

Another way of talking to the child while he plays is to use something called "descriptive commenting". You describe what the child is doing, almost like giving a running commentary. For instance: 'You are putting all the red cars together. You are making the yellow car speed along…Now it's stopped…' Try to avoid tagging questions on to the end, like 'You've put them in the garage, haven't you?'

Your comments are like a flow of positive attention, keeping the child focused on what he is doing. A steady level of descriptive commenting can be particularly helpful for children who find it hard to concentrate.

Attending: how to do it well

You can use attending in short bursts at any time through the day. Times when your child is playing or drawing are good for attending but there are plenty of other opportunities. Show the child you have noticed what he is doing by describing and commenting on small things, like how he is cleaning out his hamster cage or doing his homework.

Positive attention means more than any high-tech game. Many families fall into the trap of buying lots of expensive toys, computers and games consoles for children and expecting them to keep themselves amused. But actively joining in with the child when he is playing something simple is much more valuable.

Attending is something we do quite naturally with babies – when we use baby-talk, we describe or mirror what the baby is doing. It feels intimate, warm and rewarding for both the adult and the baby. Attending is a way of doing something similar with older children.

Attending may feel odd at first. You have to break the habit of asking questions, teaching him things or suggesting what he should do. While you are attending, you let your child take the lead and engage with him in a more responsive, creative way. You can save the teaching and instructing for other times.

If your child seems puzzled when you first start attending, just explain that you are interested in what he is doing.

Ignore any minor misbehaviour while you are attending, if you can. Turn away from him and do something else until he has started behaving properly again. Do your best to make sure he can carry on playing, but if he starts doing something seriously aggressive or destructive, you may need to put a temporary stop to things. You might say: 'Because you are scratching the table, we will have to stop playing for a few minutes'.

Sometimes it can get boring when your child wants to play the same game or do the same thing over and over again. Attending only needs to last about 10 minutes each time – and it's important to use that short period of time to fully focus on the child and what he wants to do.

A word of warning – your child may enjoy it so much when you attend that he won't want you to stop. So always give him a couple of minutes' notice that you will soon have to leave him to go and get on with your work or make a phone call – but reassure him that you will play again later or tomorrow.

Just try it out and see what happens! You won't necessarily see the benefits the first few times you do it, so keep at it. Many carers have been amazed at the changes in their children's behaviour after they have started attending regularly.

Attending: key points

- **Creative, open-ended and imaginative games work best**
- **Sit close to the child**
- **Follow and imitate the child's behaviour**
- **Notice it and describe it**
- **Make positive comments**
- **Let the child use his imagination**
- **Ignore minor misbehaviour**
- **Give a minute's warning before stopping**
- **Enjoy yourselves**

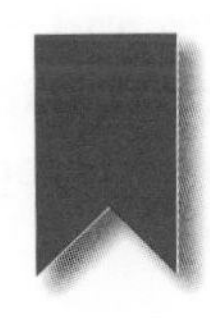

'Attending has really helped'

At first Sally, foster carer to six-year-old twins Charlie and Rosie, wasn't convinced about attending.

'Sometimes you would think it's not going to work – but gosh, it did,' she says. 'You have to give it a go and keep at it, and the results can be quite surprising.'

Sally generally attends with Charlie while he is playing with toy aeroplanes and cars or sometimes he will choose a game.

'Charlie is not into drawing but Rosie loves anything like that. She likes playing with dolls and little toys that she moves around. At first it felt a bit awkward but after a while you get used to it and it feels natural.

'When Charlie is really attention-seeking, Rosie can feel left out. But now, with attending, they wait for my sole attention – they tell each other "It'll be your turn in a minute!".

'Together with the other strategies, attending has really worked.'

Avoid spending long periods of time attending, instead, little and often is the most effective way. This week, try to do it once a day for 10 minutes each time, while your child is playing. If you can manage to do it regularly, you will start to see the benefits. If it helps, make notes here.

NOTES ABOUT ATTENDING

DAY AND TIME	ACTIVITY	HOW I FELT ABOUT IT	HOW THE CHILD RESPONDED	OTHER COMMENTS
DAY 1				
DAY 2				
DAY 3				
DAY 4				
DAY 5				
DAY 6				
DAY 7				

5 Using rewards

Praise and attention can really help a child to behave well, as we saw in Chapters 3 and 4. They act as a kind of social reward.

Sometimes praise and attention on their own are not enough, and there are a few children who don't respond particularly well to social rewards like these.

So for times when you need something extra, you can use more tangible or concrete rewards. These might include treats, small presents, pocket money or special privileges such as being allowed to stay up late.

Using tangible rewards like this is a short-term strategy – over a longer period, the social rewards will be more important for most children.

Giving rewards

There are three ways you can give rewards:

- **You can give rewards out of the blue** – for instance, when you give your child a surprise treat when she has been behaving well or has done something particularly good.
- **You can plan it in advance** so that she knows that if she completes a task or behaves in a particular way, you will give her a reward.
- **You can use a reward chart** – see pages **55–59**.

You can use rewards for:

- Helping your child to behave better and be more co-operative
- Getting rid of particular problem behaviour such as shouting or getting out of bed at night
- Encouraging your child to learn a new skill such as cleaning her teeth or getting dressed by herself
- Getting her to do certain tasks such as homework or tidying her room
- Breaking habits such as night-time wetting

What motivates your child?

Think about what your child likes doing. You will know how she chooses to spend her time, what she gets excited about and what special times or activities she looks forward to. This will give you some ideas about what you could use as rewards.

Ask your child what she likes as well – you might be surprised by some of the things she comes up with!

Make a note of them in the box opposite.

THE "WHEN...THEN..." RULE

Rewards should always be given *after* the child has done whatever it is you want her to do, not before. For instance: '*When* you have finished your homework, *then* you can play on the computer' or '*When* you have tidied your room, *then* we can go to the park'.

A reward every time?

When a child is learning to do something new, you should reward her every time she does it – whether you are using social rewards such as praise and a pat on the back, or a more tangible reward.

Later, when she has mastered it, you don't need to reward her every time – just occasionally. This will motivate her to continue the behaviour she has learned.

What my child likes

Food ____________________

Sweets/snacks ____________________

Favourite place ____________________

Favourite game ____________________

Activity ____________________

Favourite person ____________________

Special toy ____________________

Treats ____________________

Things she looks forward to ____________________

Things that cheer her up ____________________

Special times ____________________

Small gifts she would like ____________________

Any other ideas ____________________

How to make rewards work

For rewards to be really effective, they need to work in certain ways. They should be:

- **Specific**

  This means being clear about what the reward will be. Saying: 'We will do something nice' is not as effective as explaining 'I will read you a story' or 'We will have chocolate biscuits'.

- **Immediate**

  The reward should be given immediately after the behaviour you are trying to encourage. The longer the delay, the less effective the reward will be.

  Young children and children with poor concentration find it difficult to learn about the consequences of their behaviour. You have a better chance of success if you can give rewards often and straight after the behaviour – a smiley face sticker given immediately afterwards, every time, is better than a promise to buy her a treat next time you go shopping.

- **Consistent**

  Try to give rewards reliably and consistently. It is important that you notice good and appropriate behaviour and follow through with the rewards you have agreed.

- **Frequent**

  Children learn by getting plenty of feedback, so keep making the effort to praise or reward her every time, throughout the day.

- **Balanced**

  Just like the rest of us, children respond well to positive feedback. If they feel you are telling them off more often than you are praising them, they will soon get demotivated.

It could get worse before it gets better!

Some children are used to certain behaviours producing a result. For instance, they may have learned from experience that if they have a tantrum in the supermarket they will get some sweets to keep them quiet.

If you then refuse to buy the sweets when the child has a tantrum, at first her tantrums may get even worse as she tries harder and harder to produce the reward she expects – in other words, the behaviour can get worse before it gets better.

Hang on in there – behaviour that does not produce any rewards will eventually fade out. Provided you make sure there is no pay-off, the behaviour will fade away in time.

Sometimes problem behaviours do rear their ugly heads again after a little while, for no clear reason. Stand your ground and don't reward the behaviour – it will quickly fade away again.

Focus on the positive

We've all been there – there is something your child does that really bothers you and you have tried everything to get her to stop, but nothing seems to work. It seems as though you spend all your time nagging her or telling her off. Or you tell her to stop doing it and she does, but she does something else equally annoying. So it's time to try a different tack.

Rather than trying to stop a problem behaviour, the secret is to choose some other behaviour that you would like to take the place of the problem behaviour, and encourage that instead. This "target" behaviour should be one that is related to the problem behaviour but the child cannot do them both at the same time.

For instance, instead of telling your child 'Don't keep getting out of bed', you can frame it in a different way by saying 'I want you to stay in bed once you have gone to bed'. You can reward her when she achieves this.

Rather than telling your child *not* to do something, giving her a target behaviour to aim at can help you both to feel more positive. It produces behaviour which you can then encourage by giving her rewards – so it becomes a win-win situation!

Here are some examples of target behaviour.

Problem behaviour	Target behaviour
Shouting	**Talking quietly**
Kicking the cat	**Stroking the cat nicely**
Drawing on the wallpaper or other inappropriate places	**Colouring a picture**

Choosing a target behaviour

Choose a target behaviour that is fairly easy for the child to achieve. The idea is that she experiences success and then you can reward and strengthen the behaviour. Praise her as soon as she shows the slightest sign of it!

If it is too big a challenge, break it down into smaller steps – if her bedroom is really messy, expecting her to clear it all up in one go might be too much to expect. So break down the task into manageable tasks, for instance, asking her to tidy up one area of the room at a time.

Providing triggers and pay-offs for the target behaviour

You might need to think of things to do both before and after the target behaviour that will support and maintain it. For example, if you want your child to go to bed on time, you might need to establish a calming before-bedtime routine to help her settle – a bath and a bedtime story, for example. If you want her to wash her face and clean her teeth in the morning, you could put up a picture or a sign in the bathroom to prompt her.

After the behaviour you will need to reward her, for instance with praise, attention, a treat or a star for her reward chart (see **p 59**).

OVER TO YOU

CHOOSING A TARGET BEHAVIOUR

What behaviour would you like to stop?

____

____

____

____

____

____

Choose an alternative or target behaviour that you would like to see instead

____

____

____

____

____

____

Think of some triggers that might support the target behaviour

____

____

____

____

____

____

Think of some pay-offs you can give to reward the target behaviour

____

____

____

____

____

____

HOW TO INCREASE "WANTED" BEHAVIOUR

What to do beforehand

- **Turn the problem behaviour on its head – encourage an alternative positive behaviour**
- **Tell your child what you expect her to do from now on**
- **Give calm, clear instructions**
- **Use your voice and body language to show that you mean business**

Desired behaviour

What to do afterwards

- **Notice the behaviour**
- **Show your pleasure and give plenty of praise**
- **Give rewards and treats**
- **Use non-verbal rewards too – smile, wink, hug**

Reward charts

One way to use rewards is to draw up a reward chart. Each time your child does the specific behaviour you are trying to encourage, you can stick a star on the chart or colour in the appropriate space for that day.

A reward chart is a short-term way of encouraging certain behaviour and helps you to reward your child in a systematic way. It provides a structure for you to notice and reward positive behaviours.

Your child can see from the chart that she has earned a certain number of stars or stickers for doing a particular task or for learning a new skill.

Young children will be motivated by the chance of earning stickers alone, and for your praise and approval.

Older children will need other rewards, such as treats and being allowed to do certain things that they want to do. They can have these rewards when they have earned a certain number of stars or stickers.

Look back at the list on **p 50** for some possible rewards that could work with your child. Here are some examples:

- A favourite snack
- A trip to the park
- Going swimming
- Going to the cinema
- Having a friend to play

- Playing on the computer
- Spending some time with a special person, e.g. a favourite aunt
- A bedtime story
- Baking cakes
- Small gifts, e.g. a magazine, hair clips
- Being allowed to stay up late one night

For a reward chart to work well, you need to think it through carefully first and make sure you take into account your child's needs, abilities and motivation.

Get her to decorate a special folder or container to keep her tokens in. Token systems can work well with four- to seven-year-olds. With older children, you can use points rather than tokens, and keep a record of how many points the child has earned.

Using tokens

Token systems work in a similar way to star charts. They can be effective with children who need an immediate and concrete reward when they behave in the right way. When the child does what you have agreed she will do, you give her a token to reinforce the behaviour.

Just as with a reward chart, you identify a variety of rewards and decide how many tokens will be needed to earn each reward. The child can "cash in" the tokens or vouchers to earn rewards. The system can be as simple or sophisticated as you want to make it. For instance, older children might be able to cash in some tokens for small everyday rewards and save some for a bigger and longer-term reward such as a special trip.

It works best if they spend most of their tokens on short-term or medium-term rewards, such as things they will do that day or that weekend.

You might decide that your child can earn bonus tokens if she has done the task every day – for instance, if she has done some homework every night she can earn an extra token at the weekend.

The token could be, for instance, a button or even a special voucher that you have designed on the computer. Tokens are convenient and you can take them anywhere, so if your child is behaving well while you are out, you can give her tokens to reward her.

The golden rules

- **Be specific** about the behaviour you want to see. 'Be good while we are out shopping' is too general. Instead you might say, 'I want you to stay by my side when we are in the supermarket'.
- **Go for small steps.** Children work better for small goals they can achieve more easily, and they need frequent rewards. So break the task down into more manageable bits and give her a sticker or token for each bit of the task. The more you can reward success, the more she will be motivated to behave better next time.
- **Follow it through.** The reward programme will work only if you notice the "desired" behaviour and reward it straight away.

- **Pace your steps.** Once your child is managing the task, you can make it more challenging – she then has to do a little more to achieve each sticker or token.
- **Keep rewards simple.** Make them low cost or no cost.
- **Go for quick rewards.** Try not to make the rewards take too long to earn – children will give up if rewards are too slow in coming.
- **Tackle just one or two behaviours at first.** If you try to tackle too many at a time, it will be difficult for both of you. Older children may be able to work on more tasks at a time.
- **Involve your child.** Talk to her about setting up the reward programme and deciding on the rewards. She may be able to help you draw or decorate the chart too. It will work better if she sees it as something she is doing with you rather than something you are imposing on her.
- **Be flexible.** Over time you may want to change the tasks or rewards.
- **Be positive.** If your child doesn't manage a task, be upbeat and say something like: 'You didn't get any stickers today, but I'm sure you will tomorrow.'
- **Let your child keep what she has earned.** Never remove stickers, tokens or rewards as a punishment. Any discipline or punishment should be kept separate from the reward programme.
- **Make sure you're the one in charge of rewards.** Avoid leaving stickers, tokens or rewards around the house for your child to help herself to!

Over time, tangible rewards can be spaced out and eventually faded out altogether. But remember to keep on giving praise and encouragement to keep the good behaviour going.

FIVE STEPS TO DEVISING A REWARD PROGRAMME

THE BEHAVIOUR I WANT TO REWARD IS:

(Be positive, clear and specific)

____

1 **What exactly will my child need to do in order to get a sticker?** (Be specific!)

____

____

____

____

2 **When and how will I check that my child is doing this?**

____

____

____

____

3 **I expect my child to earn around ______ stickers a day**

____

____

____

____

4 **The rewards we have chosen and the number of stickers required for each reward are:**
(Make sure you discuss with your child what kind of rewards she wants to work for)

____

____

____

____

5 **Make the chart – she can help to draw it or decorate it and go with you to buy the stickers (see examples overleaf)**

Here are two sample reward charts:

OVER TO YOU

Try using the reward chart or token system for a week. To help you see how it is working, fill in your results below

DAY OF PROGRAMME	STICKERS/TOKENS/ REWARDS EARNED	COMMENTS
1		
2		
3		
4		
5		
6		
7		

If it is going well...

Well done! If your child has made good progress and has been earning lots of rewards, you might decide that it's time to move things on – perhaps by expecting her to do a little more to earn each sticker or token, or by requiring more tokens to get a reward.

For instance, suppose your goal was to get your child to eat her breakfast more quickly. If she has managed to do it in 30 minutes this week you might want to make next week's target 20 minutes. Or perhaps you want to introduce a different target behaviour into the programme now.

Revising the programme keeps it interesting and challenging.

Discuss this with your child and tell her that she is doing so well that you think she is capable of achieving even more.

If it's not going well...

If your reward programme hasn't worked as well as you had hoped, try to identify where the problem might lie. This checklist could help you see if you have all the right elements in place:

- Are you being clear and specific about the behaviour you wish to see?
- Is the behaviour too much for your child to manage? Could you break it down into smaller parts to make things a bit easier?
- Does your child understand that she is being rewarded, and what she is being rewarded for?
- Do you always notice the behaviour and reward it straight away?
- Is your child able to earn enough stickers to keep her motivated?
- Does it take her too long to earn a reward?
- Does she find the rewards fun and exciting? Or do you need to think more creatively about the rewards?
- Are you managing to apply the rewards consistently or do you sometimes forget or not have the time?
- Are you giving the rewards only when your child does what you want her to do, or do you sometimes weaken and give them anyway, even if she has not quite done the task?
- Do you give more praise and rewards than criticism in the course of a day?
- Are you giving plenty of praise and attention along with tangible rewards?
- Have you made it fun?

Changing your reward programme

Once you have looked at the results and asked yourself the questions above, write down in the box below any changes that you decide to make to your reward programme.

Discuss this with your child. Would she like to change the tasks she is working on? How does she feel about the rewards?

What we will change	We will change it to	This is why we need to make the change

Reward charts usually work best over a period of a few weeks and then they can be phased out. Naturally, you have to continue giving praise and encouragement, smiles, hugs and pats on the back!

Some goals will be achieved quickly, others will take time and patience.

Yes, you get paid for fostering, and of course caring for troubled children and making a difference to their lives can be rewarding in many ways. Sometimes you also need to give yourself a little reward or two.

Because you're worth it...

Fostering is a challenging and important role. It changes children's lives. It makes many and varied demands on you, including emotional demands, and you are almost never off duty. Yet fostering is not well-paid or high status and foster carers sometimes don't feel valued by the agencies they work with or other professionals they come into contact with.

So as a foster carer you need to acknowledge the value of what you do and take good care of your own needs – if you can do this, you will be better placed to handle the pressures and demands of the role. It's essential to make time and space for your own needs sometimes, and make it a priority to look after yourself.

Remember to look after yourself and reward yourself in other ways as well. You need to recharge your batteries on a regular basis. Everyone will have their own preferred ways of relaxing, re-energising, relieving stress or giving themselves a treat. Here are a few ideas. Which are your favourite things?

You might like to:

- Go for a walk
- Have a long bath
- Read the papers
- Watch a film
- Meet up with a friend for coffee

- Phone a friend
- Go clothes shopping
- Do some knitting
- Have a long Candy Crush Saga session
- Listen to music
- Have a massage
- Go to the gym or have a swim
- Go to the pub or a restaurant with friends or your partner
- Go to the cinema
- Go to a quiz night
- Visit an art gallery
- Go to yoga, Zumba, badminton or a dance class
- Go to a book group or choir practice
- Watch a football match
- Have a sleep
- Sit and relax in the garden with a coffee and a cream cake
- Meditate
- Attend support group or foster carer group meetings
- ...Or just sit and do nothing for a while.

Gold stars to tackle jealousy

Betty had a nine-year-old girl, Carina, placed with her. She already had another nine-year-old girl called Gemma in placement and it was clear that Carina was jealous of Gemma. Carina found it difficult when Betty gave Gemma any attention. She picked fights with Gemma and tried to bully her.

Betty set up a reward chart for Carina. If Carina did anything helpful or positive towards Gemma, she earned a gold star. When she got 10 stars, her reward was to go and stay overnight with Betty's sister, which was a special treat for her.

To avoid singling out Carina as the "difficult" child and to prevent Gemma from feeling left out, Betty also set up a reward chart for Gemma so that she could work on keeping her bedroom tidy.

'She responds so well to rewards'

Six-year-old Chantelle is hyperactive and has learning difficulties, and her behaviour presents quite a challenge for foster carer Stella.

'She can't sit down – she is always running around, diving on the sofa and throwing things,' says Stella. *'So I have a book that she calls her "Well done stickers book". She is very keen to earn points. If she can sit down for five minutes and listen to a story, she gets a sticker. When she gets upset, if she doesn't throw things around, she gets a sticker. She likes being in the kitchen, doing things, so her daily reward is to do some cooking. I give her cookery books and she chooses something she would like to cook, like fairy cakes, and we sit down and bake together.*

'She doesn't like it when she gets fewer stickers than usual. At the end of the week, if she has earned five stickers on three days, she gets £5 in her piggy bank. She is saving up for a doll's buggy. She'll say: "I've done really well!"'

'They felt good about earning rewards'

'Charlie would run up and down the aisles when we went to the supermarket and it was a real problem,' says foster carer Sally. *'So I used a sticker chart with him and his sister. As a reward, the one who had most stickers at the end of the week got to choose what we did – going to the park, going bowling or having a school friend round, little treats that made them feel special. If we ran out of stickers, we would use buttons. Rosie would earn a button if, instead of getting tearful she came and told me how she felt. She would say to me, "I didn't cry, did I?" and I would say, "No, that deserves a button".*

'At the end of the week I would make a big fuss of them and they felt good about earning these rewards. It certainly worked for these two.'

6 Listening to and talking with your child

The ability to share thoughts and feelings is an important skill for children to acquire as they grow up. Children who can manage their emotions well generally make better relationships and are better liked by both adults and peers (Goleman, 1996). Many of these skills are built and fostered through the early childhood years. Some children will not have had the kind of nurturing and supportive relationships that enable them to learn about and recognise feelings. These children may not have the vocabulary or the understanding to know what is going on inside them or how to communicate this. The inability to manage emotions can have a big impact on a child's experience at school, their ability to make and keep friendships, and their emotional and mental wellbeing.

Who do you talk to when you're upset? It is probably someone you feel close to and trust, someone who you know will help you to feel better able to manage your feelings and emotions. This is because good communication skills are at the heart of sensitive responding and helping to build good attachments.

Very young children rely on their carers to help them regulate their emotional state, for example, comforting them when they are distressed, helping them when they are frustrated because they can't do something on their own, and so on. However, there is still a role for the carer to support older children with learning to manage their emotions through sensitive and appropriate communication.

We could probably all become better listeners ourselves by working on our listening skills. We are not born with great communication skills – we have to learn them. Good communication is two-way: it starts with listening. It involves understanding what is being expressed and responding in a way that enables and encourages the other person.

Why foster carers need good communication skills

If children are given the message that their feelings are unacceptable and cannot be safely expressed, they may stop expressing them. Instead, they will internalise their emotions and become withdrawn, or express them via their behaviour.

Carers spend more time with a child than anyone else, and so are well placed to help children in managing their emotions. Carers have to take time to know and understand the children they are looking after. Talking calmly and openly is an important part of creating a positive relationship.

Good listening skills are particularly important for those caring for children, especially children who have had difficult early experiences and have had to move to live with a different family. These children need good-quality attention from their carers if they are to be able to open up and share their thoughts, feelings and previous experiences. Talking about feelings and difficult events often helps to alleviate distress. Children tend to be happier and more able to engage in life when they have someone to share things with.

Looked after children, in particular, may have had few experiences of being really listened to. They are not always able to put their feelings into words. They may be too confused, frightened or out of touch with the way they feel. So carers need to be sensitive to the messages children convey through their behaviour too. Listening well involves hearing the content of what the child says, but also requires observing and interpreting non-verbal communication – the facial expressions, tone of voice, bodily signs and behaviours that indicate how the child is really feeling. Sensitivity to the expression of feelings is an integral part of good listening.

We all have our personal value systems and we need to be aware that our religious, cultural and personal beliefs will affect the ways in which we listen and talk. Some carers may find it hard to support an emotional boy or hear a child talk critically about their parents. Other carers may not be convinced that talking about feelings is helpful. The more we are able to recognise our own beliefs, the easier it is for us to spot when these may get in the way of the needs of the child.

For most of us, there are times when we are inclined to avoid pain and smooth over difficulties. We may be tempted to tell a child not to cry rather than stick with feelings we find uncomfortable. Some children's stories are harder to listen to than others and we may be anxious about how to respond.

When a child is in difficulty or distress we often want to make them feel better or try and come up with solutions. This is a natural response and we all tend to do this, but sometimes it can be unhelpful. It may result in the child becoming frustrated and angry because his feelings have not been recognised, acknowledged and understood.

These are some of the responses to avoid:

- **Advising:** *You know what you should have done…*
- **Denying feelings:** *Don't be so upset about it.*
- **Blaming:** *Maybe you didn't think things through properly.*
- **Distracting:** *I'm sure you'll feel better about it tomorrow.*
- **Reassuring:** *I'm sure he was in a bad mood and once he's calmed down everything will be fine.*
- **Pitying:** *Oh shame! You poor thing!*
- **Psychoanalysing:** *Your real problem is that you don't have any confidence in yourself.*

Some of the communication challenges when working with looked after children

- As a foster carer, you have to respond to a variety of children's experiences ranging from everyday challenges such as falling out with school friends to experiences of loss and severe trauma. Many looked after children have to contend with separation, loss, uncertainty and worry about the future as well as painful memories.
- Communication with looked after children can be complex. First of all, you may not be aware of the child's past experiences and how these affect the way he communicates. Some children may have learned that their feelings are not acceptable and that they cannot be safely shared and expressed. How the child perceives the carer, and whether he is able to trust and confide in them, will be deeply influenced by his previous relationships.
- Each family has different rules about what feelings are acceptable, what can be talked about and what not. As a foster carer, you will need to tune in to the child's style of emotional communication. You will also need to be aware of broader cultural differences in communication style. In some cultures, touch is a very normal and acceptable aspect of communication, whereas in others it may not be. Patterns of eye contact may also be culture-specific. Maintaining eye contact with an adult could be perceived as a sign of direct and honest communication by some cultural groups, whereas others might see this as disrespectful, rude and even defiant.
- For some children, it's especially difficult to put their experiences and feelings into words: for example, children who do not have English as a first language and those

who have a learning disability. Some children will have experienced abuse and trauma and may not yet be ready or able to talk about this.

Reflective listening

Reflective listening is a little bit like attending, in that you get alongside the child and comment on what you observe. You might say something like: 'It seems to me that you feel disappointed because Zack can't come and play today' or 'It sounds like you're angry with me for saying that you have to do your homework before you can go out on your bike'. You are responding to the child's cues. But be sensitive and bear in mind that you won't always interpret the child's emotions correctly.

Reflective listening is a particular style of listening in which you are "reflecting back" to a child what you understand him to have said. It involves listening to the child from their perspective; their view of things. You are acknowledging and naming the child's feelings – something that is particularly helpful for children who have difficulty in understanding or expressing their feelings. Reflective listening can help a child to:

- accept, understand and trust their feelings;
- manage their own feelings;
- build a close relationship with you.

It also:

- increases self-esteem;
- leaves responsibility with the child;
- encourages the child to share more.

How it's done

- Stop what you are doing and give the child your full attention.
- Listen to the feelings, not just the problem.
- When there is a pause, repeat back what you think your child has said or feels.
- Use open questions (i.e. questions that don't just require a "yes" or "no" answer).
- Pay attention to your tone of voice, facial gesture and body posture – these should convey interest and warmth without being overbearing.
- Resist interrupting – give the child a chance to say what it is he wants to say.
- Try and see things from the child's perspective.
- Encourage the child to continue and say more – 'tell me more'.

To enhance your awareness of listening skills, next time you are watching a soap or a drama series on television, analyse what a few of the characters do when having a conversation with someone. How many of the things on the above list are they doing? Are they a good listener – or a terrible one? Are they responding in a helpful or unhelpful way?

Talking about feelings

How to help children learn to identify, accept and share feelings

- Provide a warm, calm, nurturing environment.

Remember, although we cannot alter a child's temperament, we can help them learn how to regulate their emotions.

- Feelings are always valid – accept your child's emotions.
- Avoid letting your own beliefs and prejudices get in the way of accepting children's feelings, for example, thinking that they should always be respectful when talking about their parents.
- Try to find out how your child feels; avoid telling your child what he feels.
- Think aloud your own feelings and coping strategies.
- Read books and watch TV programmes together and use puppets and play to help make feelings part of the conversations you have with the child.
- Praise your child when they express and/or manage their emotions and calm themselves down.
- Coach your child through their emotions.

How to respond when your child talks about feelings

- Be non-judgemental and non-blaming. Many looked after children will feel responsible, in some way, for some of the bad things that have happened to them and possibly others. It is common for children who have been abused, for example, to internalise the blame and guilt for these events and to feel "bad" or at fault. They may therefore need repeated reassurance and affirmation to help them feel loved and lovable.
- Use touch sensitively.
- Go at the child's pace – be sensitive to their cues.
- If a child says, 'I'm so angry with Adam I'm going to belt him,' you can accept the child's feelings but not how they intend to act on them. Receive, accept and acknowledge his anger and frustration (when he expresses it). When he is calmer you can be clear that it is unacceptable to act this out.

Carers can model how to share both positive and difficult feelings. This will help children to learn that it is OK to feel sad and angry, and that it is possible to manage these feelings without abusing or damaging other people. This is an important message to learn.

Name or validate a child's feeling

- Naming feelings can help children identify their emotions. This helps them to understand what is happening for them. For example:
  - *That must have been disappointing for you!*
  - *Sounds as if you are pretty resentful about...*
  - *I know it's scary, but...*
  - *Wow, you sound happy!*

ASKING QUESTIONS

Asking questions is an important and basic skill and conveys interest in the person we are communicating with. It is worth reflecting on how we can best do this.

The way we ask questions has an impact on how the child responds. Sometimes questions can be inhibiting and threatening. Many children don't have much to say when asked, 'What did you do at school today?' Sometimes it is helpful to ask a more specific question like, 'What did you do in literacy hour this morning?' or 'What did you play at break?'

Question types to avoid

- Avoid general questions that may be hard to answer.
- Avoid "why" questions as these are generally unproductive. Children rarely know the answer to the question "why" and are likely to feel pressurised and blamed.
- Avoid closed questions – those that require only a "yes" or "no" answer – as they tend to inhibit the flow of conversation.
- Avoid leading questions, as these suggest a particular response and so they can inhibit the child from saying what they really feel and think. For example, if a child is asked, 'Are you feeling happy?' It may be difficult for them to actually say 'no!'.

Try these ways of helping your child to express himself.

- Use specific questions like: 'What did you have for lunch?'
- Ask open questions to encourage the child to talk: 'What happened next?'; 'What was it like to meet your aunt?'
- Sometimes it's best to avoid questions and, instead, use descriptive commenting, which can be less threatening; for example, 'You look sad', or 'You look really happy'.
- If a child tends to be negative, you might want to frame questions that will get a positive response, such as: 'What was the best thing that happened today?'

Managing emotions

If you become skilled in reflective listening, asking questions well and helping your child to understand and express his feelings, as outlined above, you can make a difference to how he manages his emotions. It's also important for carers to encourage their children's positive emotions.

Stress and anxiety often make us focus on the negatives – this is true for ourselves and also for our children. Sometimes we may not even notice the positive things that happen or that children manage to achieve – such as finding a constructive way to express their anger rather than trashing their room, or coming to ask for comfort rather than self-harming.

Remember, if you consistently notice and praise a child for behaving in the right way, over time the behaviour is more likely to happen more frequently.

Over the course of this week, look for opportunities to praise your child whenever he has successfully managed to express his feelings appropriately or to calm down after an incident that left him feeling stressed, anxious or angry.

Make a note of what happened and how you praised the child.

Day	What happened/ how child felt/what child did	What I said/ did	How child responded	Comments/ observations
Monday				
Tuesday				
Wednesday				
Thursday				
Friday				
Saturday				
Sunday				

The importance of identity

What are the things that make up your identity? They will include things like your gender, ethnic origin, where you grew up, your social class, appearance, your roles, e.g. mother, father, foster carer, and things that are important to you, e.g. if you support a particular political party or are a keen cook or gardener. Your identity also includes your aspirations for the future.

We all have different facets to our identity – some of these are obvious to others while some are less noticeable but nonetheless important to us.

Foster carers need to show the children they care for that they value them for who they are, and help them to develop a positive sense of their own identity.

For children who have been separated or removed from the families they were born into, though, questions of identity can be complicated. Their identity has been formed in a family which, temporarily at least, they are no longer living with. The child has become "a child in care", a "looked after child". This will affect the way they see themselves and the way others see them.

Some children in care, of course, will go on to be adopted and this can create even more complex issues around identity for them. Foster carers can prepare and encourage them to see themselves as being part of two or more family groups and experience the richness of this in their lives.

Children in foster families may have more difficulty than their peers in creating a secure sense of identity and "narrative" about their life. They may not fully understand the reasons why they are in foster care. Some may even blame themselves and think it is because they were bad or unlovable.

Some children may want to talk about these issues, their family and their past experiences, while others may give the impression that it is a "closed door" and that they do not want or need to talk about it. As a foster carer, you need to convey an attitude of openness and acceptance, showing that you are willing to listen if the child wants to talk about these things. Ensure that discussions about different families, "belonging", the past, where children come from, information about their heritage, culture and ethnicity are alive and part of everyday life. Use your reflective listening skills and the other skills discussed in this chapter to validate the child's feelings, both positive and negative. The child's feelings are always valid.

Be realistic and truthful when the child wants to talk about their family or the possibility of returning home or even being adopted.

7 How to be good at giving instructions

KEEP INSTRUCTIONS SIMPLE

When you ask your child to put her dirty plate in the sink, go to bed or pick up her coat and hang it up, does she refuse, argue or simply ignore you? The way you ask a child to do something is important because it can make it either more or less likely that she will do as she is told.

This chapter will give you ideas on improving the way you communicate with your child when you are giving instructions.

Don't expect too much

Of course, no child does as she is told 100 per cent of the time – that would be an unrealistic expectation. Just like the rest of us, children have their own priorities and preferences and they don't want to do what someone else tells them all the time. Many looked after children come from families where there are no rules, or where adults apply rules inconsistently, and they have been able to do more or less what they want.

So carers need to set up new patterns of managing everyday interactions with the child, which will influence how co-operative she is likely to be.

How things can go wrong

A lot of conflict in families arises from everyday interactions that go wrong – simple requests or instructions that escalate into a full-blown argument or confrontation. Children can be very good at avoiding things they don't want to do. They may have learned that if they shout and complain enough, the adult will not follow through on his or her instructions and they can get away without doing whatever it is they were told to do. In these situations the child's inappropriate behaviour (ignoring, complaining or shouting) is rewarded because she avoids having to do what she was asked to do.

With a child like this, some carers become more and more reluctant to give instructions because they know the child is likely to make a scene or refuse to do as she is told. This might make life easier for the adult in the short term, but in the longer term it makes matters worse as it teaches the child that behaving badly pays off, and they also avoid learning about the skills and responsibilities that are part of growing up.

The other thing that often happens is that the adult gets frustrated and decides to make a stand. He or she starts to shout and make threats to try and force the child to give in. This rather threatening and aggressive behaviour might have the effect of making the child obey, but in the long term it doesn't help anyone. The adult feels that the only way to get the child to behave is to shout and threaten, and children pick up the message that you can get your way by being aggressive and threatening.

How NOT to give instructions

Researchers have identified six common mistakes many of us make when we are giving instructions to children. When we make these mistakes, children are *less* likely to do as they are told.

- **Too many instructions.** Bombarding a child with instructions can overwhelm her and makes it less likely that she will comply.
- **Chain instructions.** When you string a lot of instructions together – 'I want you to pick up your books from the floor, put the videos straight, put the chairs back where they were and take your bag upstairs' – it makes it difficult for the child to

remember everything. She is almost bound to forget one or two of the instructions, so will fail to do everything you asked.

- **Vague instructions.** When you say things like 'Be careful' or 'That's enough', you know what you want but the child does not necessarily understand. Some of us feel uncomfortable telling a child what to do, so we make statements like 'Your coat is on the floor' when what we really mean is 'Please pick up your coat and hang it up now'.
- **Framing instructions as questions.** Asking questions like 'Would you like to put your toys away now?' or 'Are you ready for your bath?' blurs the distinction between a question and an instruction. It provides the option for the child to say 'No', which is not what you want to hear!
- **Giving an instruction followed by an explanation.** This makes your instruction less clear. It makes it easier for your child to get you into an argument about it, which will distract you from the issue. It's better to give your explanation first, followed by a clear instruction.
- **"Let's..."** instructions. Don't say things like 'Let's get ready for bed' if you have no intention of getting into your own pyjamas! The child will feel you have misled her.

Remember your body language

It's not only what you say that counts, it's the way you say it. The child will be more likely to take you seriously if your non-verbal behaviour shows you mean business:

- Stand, rather than sit, when you give your child an instruction.
- Get within arm's length of the child and make eye contact.
- Use the child's name.
- Speak firmly and clearly.

HOW IT'S DONE

When giving instructions, do the following.

- Choose your time carefully. Most children hate to be interrupted when they are absorbed in a game or a programme. If you can, wait until a child has finished what she's doing or there is a break.
- Get close to the child and get her attention.
- Tell her what to do.
- Wait five seconds for her to do what you've asked.
- If she co-operates, praise her.
- If she doesn't do what you have asked, repeat your instruction. Again, wait five seconds for her to comply. Warn her that you will use a specified consequence if she doesn't co-operate (see Chapter 10 for more about consequences).
- If she co-operates, praise her. If not, use the back-up consequence.

GIVING CLEAR AND CALM INSTRUCTIONS: THE KEY POINTS

Remember the ABC analysis of behaviour? Your instruction is like the antecedent or trigger. The way we give instructions has a big impact on the way the child responds.

1 **Get her attention.** Get your child to listen to you by making eye contact, using her name and speaking slowly and clearly yet firmly.

2 **Be brief.** Long explanations will just encourage her to question you or argue.

3 **Be clear.** Make sure your child knows exactly what you want her to do: 'Move your cup further onto the table' is better than 'Be careful!'

4 **Be positive.** Tell her what to do rather than what not to do. 'Please speak quietly' is better than 'Stop shouting'.

5 **Give one instruction at a time.** Allow her to do what you asked and praise her before you tell her to do anything else.

6 **Be polite.** We often betray our annoyance or criticism by the tone of our voice or our choice of words ('How many times have I told you to...?'). Try to avoid putting the child down.

7 **Be realistic.** For instance, if a child has poor concentration and you tell her to spend 30 minutes alone doing her homework, she won't be able to manage it. Only ask her to do things she is capable of doing.

8 **Give warnings and reminders.** If a child is wrapped up in a game or programme, it can be helpful to give a warning that you are going to want her to do something soon: 'When this programme ends you must go to bed.' This provides time for the child to get used to the idea.

9 **Give options.** If you are going to stop a child doing something she enjoys, try to provide an alternative: 'You can't play with your ball in the house, but you can set the train set out instead if you like.'

10 **Avoid arguments.** Ignore the child's protests and arguments. Giving attention will just reward these. You can provide explanations at another time if you need to.

11 **Give "When...then..." instructions.** With older children, you may want to give them some choice over whether to comply or not. Offer an incentive for the child to do what you ask, while implying that she has a choice: 'When you have done your reading, then you can watch some television.'

12 **Follow through with praise or a consequence.** If the child co-operates, reward her. Praising her encourages her to co-operate next time. But if the child refuses to do what you ask, don't just ignore this – you must follow it through – otherwise she will learn to ignore your instructions. If she doesn't do as she is told, there must be some consequences.

'I learned not to shout'

Stella says: 'The Fostering Changes *course was very helpful in that before, I would have shouted more at Chantelle. Shouting just makes the child scared of the adult. Now, I take my time explaining. I give a warning and count to three. She will say "All right" and do it.*

'I can see real progress. Before, she wouldn't stop what she was doing to even look at you when you spoke to her. Now she will stop, look at you and listen and give you an answer.'

'I talk to her more calmly now'

Heather says that, before attending the* Fostering Changes *course, she used to make mistakes with three-year-old Sarah. She feels that a lot of mothers do the same thing when they are tired or stressed and the kids are getting on their nerves.

'Instead of telling them something quietly and calmly, you shout "Put that down! Don't do that! Come here!" and you don't realise you are giving them too much information and they can't take it all in. Going on the course helped me look at myself and be calmer when I'm talking to her.

'It's better to give an instruction and try not to push it all at once. For example, sometimes there are toys all over the place in Sarah's room. I used to shout to her from outside her room: "Pack away your toys, put your shoes away, pick those up, put that in the cupboard..."

'Now I go down to her level, I make sure we have eye contact and I say: "Sarah, pack away your toys". Sometimes it might take a bit of time but I would come to her, look at her and say it again. I found it very helpful. Obviously I couldn't change her overnight, but her response was good.'

8 Using "selective ignoring" to improve behaviour

Up to now in this programme, we have been looking at skills that encourage and reward a child. But what can you do when a child continues to display negative behaviour?

This chapter looks at a strategy that you can use to discipline a child. It works particularly well with behaviours where the child is playing up largely to get attention.

HERE'S HOW IT WORKS

Jamie is drawing with his carer. He starts throwing his pencils on the floor. His carer ignores this – she turns away, not speaking to him or looking at him any more. As soon as he carries on drawing or picks up a pencil, the carer turns back round to him and says: 'You've picked up a pencil. Good boy. And now you're drawing some beautiful green grass. I like that.'

For a child, attention is a very powerful motivator. Much of children's behaviour is strengthened when adults pay attention to it. Positive attention from an adult acts as a reward.

However, some children have such a deep need for adult attention that they will do whatever they can to get it, even if the attention comes in the form of criticism, shouting and telling off.

Use your attention as a "reward" for appropriate behaviour. Withdraw your attention – so that there is no pay-off – when the child's behaviour is inappropriate.

This can happen when children have learned that adults ignore them when they are quiet or behaving appropriately. In this situation, children quickly learn that the best way to get attention from adults is to play up and misbehave. This may be the experience your child had before he came to you.

Many of us do resort to shouting at children and telling them off when we are under pressure. This means we are rewarding misbehaviour by giving it our attention, rather than correcting it. It is much better for the child to learn that if he behaves appropriately, he will get the attention he wants.

Ignoring misbehaviour is one of the ways you can influence the way he behaves.

For instance, if a child realises that making silly noises gets him no attention but talking in his normal voice means his carer will pay attention and listen to him, he will soon stop making silly noises.

Target positive behaviour

Simply ignoring the behaviour won't tell the child how he should behave – we also need to target the positive behaviour we want to see and provide rewards for that.

Who gets the attention?

Two children are eating their lunch. One is playing with her food and throwing it around. The other is getting on with eating. Many adults will automatically tell off the child who is messing with her food. But why not use your attention more strategically? Ignore the child who is messing about with her food and give praise and attention to the child who is getting on with eating.

WHAT BEHAVIOUR CAN YOU IGNORE?

There are lots of annoying but fairly harmless behaviours that you can safely ignore. For instance:

- Moaning
- Whining
- Silly noises and voices
- Nail-biting
- Pulling faces
- Complaining
- Minor squabbles
- Fiddling
- Tantrums
- Rudeness
- Swearing
- Messy eating
- Nose-picking

Which behaviour is not suitable?

Obviously, if the child is doing something dangerous to himself or others or being destructive, you will need to put a stop to it straight away – so ignoring it is out of the question. And there may be other things your child does that you personally find so stressful or difficult that you know you won't be able to manage to ignore them. Ignoring works best with minor irritating behaviours.

Ignoring should never be a way of expressing your own feelings

Some carers are struggling with feelings of frustration, anger and disappointment and can fall into the trap of very obviously "ignoring" the child as a way of showing how they feel. Take care to use ignoring only as a very specific and focused way of withdrawing your attention from certain behaviour, for as long as the behaviour lasts.

Isn't it cruel to ignore a child?

Ignoring should never be used as a punishment. You should use it selectively, to withdraw attention from minor irritating behaviour. Ignoring the child for long periods is unfair and unkind.

Only ignore one or two behaviours – target any more than this, and you will be spending too long ignoring the child and he will start to feel neglected.

What's so good about ignoring?

- The child gets no attention when he behaves badly, so bad behaviour goes unrewarded.
- It is a great alternative to nagging, shouting and so on – it can help you feel calmer.
- It keeps a positive relationship with the child.
- It makes you a good role model for the child – you demonstrate the art of keeping your cool in the face of provocation!

SELECTIVE IGNORING: HOW TO DO IT

Ignoring involves not making eye contact, not speaking to or touching the child, and turning away from him.

- Decide which behaviours you are going to ignore (don't choose anything that stresses you out too much).
- Explain to the child what you are going to do.
- Be sure you are prepared to see things through.
- When you are ignoring the child, be subtle and neutral, not dramatic (don't laugh/smile at the child's antics).
- Be consistent in your use of ignoring.
- Limit how often and for how long you use it.
- Combine ignoring with distractions.
- Use ignoring together with praise and attention for appropriate behaviour.

Choose one or two behaviours that you will ignore over the next week. Make a note of the behaviours here.

Behaviour I will ignore:

1 ______________________________

____

____

____

____

____

2 ______________________________

____

____

____

____

____

Use the charts below to make a note of when you use the strategy and what effect it has. Make a mark in column 2 every time the behaviour occurs on that day.

Tip for carers: get on with tidying up, reading the newspaper, or talking with someone else when you are ignoring the child. You may need to keep yourself calm by making coping, positive statements.

BEHAVIOUR 1:

DAY	HOW MANY TIMES THE BEHAVIOUR OCCURS	TOTAL	EFFECT OF IGNORING
1			
2			
3			
4			
5			
6			
7			

BEHAVIOUR 2:

DAY	HOW MANY TIMES THE BEHAVIOUR OCCURS	TOTAL	EFFECT OF IGNORING
1			
2			
3			
4			
5			
6			
7			

DID YOU FIND...

- **...the behaviour got worse before it got better? This is because at first the child may misbehave even more in an attempt to gain your attention. See it through! Sooner or later he will realise that it doesn't work – and that the way to get your attention is to behave well.**
- **...the number of times the behaviour was occurring in a day had reduced by the end of the week? This is evidence of your success – ignoring a particular behaviour makes the child less likely to repeat it.**

STILL STRUGGLING?

- **Try using more distraction. For instance, ignore the fact that the child is picking an argument with his sister and suggest that he helps you put out the bread and cakes for tea instead.**
- **Remember to combine ignoring with attending and lots of praise. Ignoring only works when the child experiences the contrast between ignoring and positive, warm attention.**
- **Make sure no-one else in the household is providing a pay-off for the behaviour that you are ignoring. Remove the child to a quiet place if you have to.**

'I stopped reacting'

Six-year-old Peter and his eight-year-old brother David had suffered chronic and serious neglect. One of Peter's problem behaviours when he was placed with foster carer Colleen was that he would urinate around the house.

Colleen says: 'I was always having to think on my feet because he was always one step ahead of me – the Fostering Changes *course gave me new ideas on how to manage things. I used ignoring a lot more. When he urinated, I stopped reacting – I would just say "OK" and calmly ask him to help clean it up. I didn't question him about why he had done it, which I would have done before. He looked quite taken aback – it surprised him.'*

9 Setting limits

Many looked after children have lived with adults who have never set any boundaries for them or who have been inconsistent. This means they have missed out on the chance to develop a sense of inner stability and self-control.

As a carer, you can make up for this to some extent. You can provide care, warmth, sensitive responding and praise. You can also provide guidelines to provide safety and protection for the child, to contain her sometimes challenging behaviour and to help her learn how to get along with other people.

All children naturally want to do their own thing and don't always do as they are told – this can be seen as a healthy sign of independence. When children hardly ever do as they are told, life can become frustrating and exhausting for their carers.

This chapter looks at setting limits and boundaries for children. Chapter 10 will look at what to do when children cross those boundaries and misbehave.

Discipline

We all have our own ideas about what "discipline" means and what we expect from a child. We all have our own disciplinary style – some believe in being firm but fair, others are warmer and less strict. Most of us are flexible and our styles vary depending on the situation and the needs of the child.

Looked after children: why discipline is different

When it comes to discipline, there are some issues that apply when working with looked after children that don't necessarily apply with your own children. For instance:

- You have to comply with your fostering agency's guidelines on control, restraint and discipline.
- Fostering legislation in the UK makes it clear that smacking, slapping and other forms of corporal punishment are not acceptable.
- Social workers have their own personal and professional values and judgments that may not be the same as yours (or even the agency's). As a carer, you can sometimes be given unclear or mixed messages, which makes it harder to know what to do in some situations.
- Some carers feel vulnerable to child protection allegations – they feel that if they take a firm line on discipline, it could be misconstrued and used against them.
- Carers are also only too aware that some looked after children have experienced physical and emotional abuse. They may fear that the child's previous experience will affect the way she feels when they have to discipline her.

Safe caring

In the context of foster caring, "safe caring" means relating to the child in a way that is:

- Safe and respectful for the child; and
- Safe for foster carers, in that they do not lay themselves open to misunderstandings or to allegations of abuse.

The strategies in this programme represent "safe caring". They involve treating the child with respect. They allow carers to plan their responses in advance, to respond in more rational and consistent ways, and to avoid heated and impulsive reactions.

These are the principles of the programme, which are consistent with safe caring.

- The carer explains the strategies calmly in advance, at a neutral moment, so the child knows what will happen if she behaves in a certain way.
- The carer makes sure the child knows why she is going to use this approach.
- Discipline is most effective when it is used in a calm, rational and consistent way, not in a state of anger or heightened emotion.

- When a child's behaviour is particularly difficult or challenging, carers will need support – they may need to discuss with the agency the strategies they are using and the reasons for them.
- Carers have to be scrupulously fair about the child's rights – if they take anything from the child as a consequence for misbehaviour, such as money or a possession, they will need to put it in safe keeping.
- Carers need to keep records of the child's behaviour and the strategies they are using, particularly in situations of conflict.

It is easier for children to behave well if they know what is expected of them. Looked after children who come to you may be used to very different standards of behaviour from those of your family. So drawing up some family rules is a good idea – it tells them how you expect them to behave.

Family rules

Everyone has their own priorities – good table manners might be a big issue for one carer but completely unimportant to another.

How to come up with your rules

- Think about the things that matter to you and the rest of the family, including the child herself.
- Get the whole family together to discuss and agree on the rules.
- Decide on five to ten rules.
- Make them clear and brief.
- If you can, make the rules say what everyone should, rather than should not, do: 'Keep your hands and feet to yourself' rather than 'Don't hit or kick people'.
- The rules should be about behaviour you can observe – for instance, you can't see what happens at school or at the football club.

How to make the rules work well

- Write the rules down and pin them up on the wall.
- Make it clear that the rules apply to everyone in the house.

If a child breaks a rule...

- Get the child's attention.
- Explain that she has broken a rule and why that is a problem.
- Get the child to explain what she should have done.
- Tell her to do it.
- Praise her when she does it correctly.

Suppose there is a rule that you eat food only in the kitchen. You find your child is eating a bowl of cereal in the living room. Here's what you do:

- Get the child's attention.
- Simply and calmly tell her what the problem is: 'You have taken your cereal into the living room.'
- Say briefly why that is a problem: 'You could spill it on the sofa or the carpet.'
- Ask the child to tell you the appropriate behaviour: 'We are meant to eat in the kitchen.'
- Ask her to do it.
- Praise her for the right behaviour: 'Thank you for taking your cereal back to the kitchen to eat.'

Here's an example of one family's rules.

THE RULES AT 10 MARKHAM PLACE

We always try to tell the truth and be polite.

We always ask permission before taking things that belong to other people.

After eating, we take our plates out to the kitchen.

We speak kindly to the animals and always treat them gently.

We change out of our uniforms and put play clothes on when we come home from school.

We wash every day and clean our teeth after breakfast and after dinner.

We flush the toilet after we use it.

Rules and boundaries for keeping children safe online

The use of the internet and social networking is something that all families have to consider. How can children benefit from everything the online world has to offer while still being as safe as possible? How can parents and carers manage the risks?

It's a subject well beyond the scope of this book, but there are many helpful websites full of useful information on all aspects of internet safety, including videos to watch with your child or teenager, advice on how to use privacy settings and how to set parental controls on various devices, and tips on how to deal with cyberbullying and how to talk about difficult subjects such as "sexting". For starters, have a look at these sites:

- www.thinkuknow.co.uk
- www.theparentzone.co.uk
- www.saferinternet.org.uk

You might also like to read *Foster Care and Social Networking*, by Eileen Fursland (2010), published by BAAF. This deals with the question of contact between children in foster care and their families, as well as other internet safety issues.

When it comes to setting limits around the child's use of the internet and social networking, this is something foster carers need to discuss with the child's social worker to determine what is necessary and appropriate. Ideally, before the child comes into the placement, you will want to know what devices the child is bringing with her; what filtering and parental control settings (if any) have been applied; whether the child has a history of problems related to internet use – for example, has she been bullied online or has she bullied others; has she ever gone to meet anyone she's "met" online, etc; and what rules and boundaries she needs in the placement.

You will need to have a discussion with the child and the social worker (and possibly also the child's parent) about what she should and should not be allowed to do. You will want to listen and gain the child's understanding and agreement about rules for using the internet and social networking in your home. You can explain that you have a set of family rules that apply to everyone in the household (e.g. what kind of websites and online behaviour are off limits; reporting it if you encounter illegal or harmful content) and then a separate agreement that is appropriate for each child's age and individual needs.

Setting boundaries: what to include in your rules and agreements

- Using "safe search" mode, filtering software and child-friendly search engines
- Use of parental controls on laptops, mobiles, games consoles, internet-enabled televisions, etc.
- Connecting to the internet – what wifi connection to use
- The monitoring/reporting tools you will be using (if any) to supervise the child's use of the internet
- Limits on how much time the child can spend online/playing games
- Using social networking sites – which ones can the child use? Who can they talk to?
- "Friending" on social networking sites
- Using privacy setting on social networking sites and (if necessary) how to avoid being traced
- Sharing – what personal information must not be shared and what precautions are needed
- Online games – which ones can the child use?
- What is the child not allowed to do, e.g. downloading material illegally, online gambling, etc.?
- How to behave responsibly and appropriately online
- Sharing photographs – what type of photographs and with whom? Does she understand the risks of sharing self-generated sexual images ("sexting")?
- Viewing or sharing inappropriate content including hate websites and violent video clips

- Cyberbullying – what to do, whom to tell
- Risks of online grooming – recognising signs, what to do, whom to tell (reassure the child that she won't get into trouble if she tells you even if she has done or said something unwise)
- Sanctions for breaking the rules could include not allowing her to play computer or online games or use the internet for a short time.

If you suspect that the child is having secret online contact with someone they are not meant to be in contact with, tell the child's social worker.

Supervising and monitoring

- Be interested and be positive, even if you find it all quite worrying! Learn as much as you can, and ask the child to show you her favourite sites and games and to demonstrate how things work – like the privacy settings – if she's more expert than you. You don't have to become an expert in the technology – using your communication skills and building trust are just as important.
- If a child has been allowed freedom to do whatever she wants online until now, having rules and boundaries may come as a shock. Explain why rules are necessary and why you need to be involved in this aspect of her life. Be willing to listen and review the rules in the light of how the child behaves.
- Remember that technological solutions, such as filtering and monitoring and parental controls, only go so far – they are not foolproof and you simply cannot control everything your child does online. Use them when appropriate, but remember that there is no substitute for you, the child's carer, listening and talking to her about her online life and discussing with her how to stay safe and keep things positive.
- It is possible to use technological tools to "spy" on the child but this will introduce an element of secrecy and distrust into your relationship. In most cases it is not appropriate. There are benefits to the child in your actions being open, and in her knowing that you are caring for her and supervising her.
- Remember that even if you supervise what she can view at home or on her own mobile phone, there are other places she can access the internet, for example, friends' houses, friends' mobile phones. But don't let this make you feel helpless. You can still create rules, take a stand, and show the child you care about what she does and what happens to her online.
- You will need to have some discussions about sensitive subjects, for example, about why it's not a good idea to watch disturbing or distressing videos even if all her friends are watching them; why sexting can lead to huge problems for young people; and why online pornography is misleading and damaging. If you need to, find out more about these subjects on the e-safety websites for parents and carers.
- Make sure the child or young person knows she can always tell you if someone is bothering her, harassing her or even blackmailing her online. Reassure her that she won't get into trouble and you won't stop her from using the internet or her mobile phone – but you do want to know, so that you can help.

Online contact

Some children in foster care are not meant to have any contact with certain people who pose a risk to them. Make sure your child understands how to reduce the risk of being traced and found online – she may need to be particularly careful about what she shares, and with whom, on social networking sites. She needs to be careful not to inadvertently give away information about her location, for example, via location-sharing apps and digital photographs. Ask her to tell you if anyone she is not meant to have contact with approaches her online.

MY IDEAS FOR SOME FAMILY RULES

Before you have a family discussion, start thinking about what you would like to include in the rules for your own family. Make some notes here.

- **Have a family discussion. Have a large sheet of paper in front of you so you can jot down everyone's thoughts and ideas.**
- **When you have all agreed on what the rules will be, write them down on the next page.**
- **You could get the child to design and produce a poster showing the rules, which you can stick up on the wall at home.**
- **See the family rules as "work in progress". After you have lived with the rules for a while you may decide you need to fine-tune or change them!**

Our family rules

Set some rules for yourself too!

This chapter has been about family rules. Why not think about setting some rules for yourself too? Think about what rules might help you to look after yourself and consider your own needs. These rules will be different for everyone. Put your list up somewhere where you will see it and be reminded. Here are some ideas – but you should come up with your own list of the rules that would help you the most.

- I will not beat myself up for things that are not my fault.
- I will make sure I have some time to myself each week to do something I enjoy.
- I will look back on each day and try to find at least one thing to be thankful for.
- I will make time to meditate or practise mindfulness most days of the week.
- When I need it, I will ask my partner/mum/dad/best friend/supervising social worker for help.
- When I'm getting stressed I will take a step back and begin again, asking myself "what is important here?"

Telling the child how her behaviour makes you feel

Don't overdo the use of "I..." messages. Use them too often and they will lose their impact and overburden the child with too much information about your feelings.

Sometimes children can behave in ways that leave us feeling angry, frustrated, upset, rejected or taken for granted. When we feel like this, the danger is that we give vent to our feelings by giving negative attention to the child in the form of telling her off, nagging her or losing our temper.

Discipline is most effective when we can do it calmly, without letting our negative feelings enter into it.

It's important for carers to have their own support networks – perhaps their partner or a sympathetic friend or group – so they can offload feelings like this. Talking about feelings with someone else means you are less likely to blow your top with the child.

But there are some times when it can be helpful to let the child know that you have needs and feelings too. There is a way to do this, calmly and assertively, without hurting or verbally attacking the child. And that is by giving an "I..." message. An "I..." message lets you take responsibility for your own feelings. It tells her how you feel, but without accusing or blaming her.

The usual way to do this is to say: 'When you (behave in a certain way), I feel.... because...' and then add: 'I would like...' Letting the child know what you want them to do instead is helpful especially if the child doesn't know or isn't clear.

For instance:

Message that lays blame on the child

'Your language is appalling and you never show me any respect.'

'You treat this place like a hotel and I'm not your servant!'

"I..." message

'When you swear at me, I feel really hurt because it seems as though you have no respect for me.'

'When you come in and drop your coat on the floor, I feel as though you are taking me for granted because I have to clear up after you.'

'I would like you to speak to me in a polite way or hang up your coat when you come in.'

Think about some of the times when you have told off the child (or someone else – this works with partners too!).

See if you can say the same thing, this time using an "I..." message instead. An "I..." message tells the child how her behaviour makes you feel. If it helps, write it down here.

What I said	What I could have said ('When you ... I feel ... because ...' 'I would like...')

10 Helping children learn from the consequences of their actions

This and the following chapter will give you two different strategies you can use when you need to discipline the child. They are a positive alternative to shouting and making threats, which some carers sometimes resort to when they are feeling low, tired and stressed. Shouting and threats tend to make most situations worse.

These positive strategies are:

- Natural and logical consequences (for minor repeated misbehaviour)
- Time-out from positive reinforcement – sometimes just called time-out for short (for more serious and negative misbehaviour).

First, you have to work on your relationship...

These strategies can only work in the context of a positive relationship, where you have already established some kind of trust and bond with the child. So the first step is to create as positive, warm and rewarding a relationship with the child as you can. The strategies outlined in Chapters 3 and 4 (on praise and positive attention) will help you do this.

LEARNING FROM THE RESULTS OF OUR ACTIONS

We all learn about the world by observing the results of things we do – in other words, the consequences of our actions.

As children grow up, carers need to allow them to experience the consequences of their actions so that they learn about the world and develop their own sense of personal responsibility and competence.

However, we also need to nurture and protect them. We don't want them to learn from experience of the dangers of boiling water, electrical appliances and road traffic. With young children, we have to intervene when the consequence would be dangerous.

Natural consequences

Some consequences can be described as natural consequences – in other words, they are what happens when adults or others do not intervene to protect children from the results of their actions. As long as there is no danger involved, we may feel it is helpful and informative for the child to learn from certain actions:

- If he walks in puddles without wellies, he will get wet feet.
- If he doesn't eat his lunch, he will feel hungry by dinnertime.

Logical consequences

"Logical consequences" are consequences designed by carers and other adults as suitable consequences for certain behaviours. For instance:

- If the child plays football in the house, the carer will take his ball away.
- If he deliberately breaks his sister's toy, he will have to replace it out of his own pocket money.
- If he refuses to wipe his feet and brings mud into the house, he will have to clear it up.
- If he is late for school, he gets a detention.

The child is held accountable for his behaviour and experiences a consequence that is mildly unpleasant as a result.

Using logical consequences with children

Looked after children with challenging behaviour, like any other children, need to learn about the consequences of their behaviour. If there are no negative consequences when they misbehave, they may well carry on behaving in ways that are inappropriate, anti-social and self-destructive.

Carers can come up with logical consequences that they can apply as a response to a child's undesirable behaviour.

Most of us prefer to avoid conflict if we can. However, disciplining children *does* involve conflict, but as adults and carers we do need to help children learn that if they misbehave, there will be consequences. Letting children "get away with it" does not do them any favours in the long term.

You can use simple logical consequences even with children as young as two. You can use an 'If…then…' sentence to explain it to them: 'If you throw your food around, then I will take it away.'

Doing this:

- Holds the child accountable for what he does
- Helps him make the link between his behaviour and the consequences.

Guidelines for natural and logical consequences

- **Discuss the consequences in advance**

  Warn the child of the consequences of his behaviour beforehand. He needs to know that if he does not do his homework, he will not be allowed to play on the computer, rather than having this sprung on him: 'You haven't done your homework, so you can't play on the computer.' This reduces the risk of the child attributing the consequence to the wrong reason, e.g. 'The carer doesn't like me' or 'She's just mean' or 'She thinks I'm lazy'. When children know about the consequences in advance, they have a chance to decide how they want to respond. This helps them learn to take responsibility for their decisions – and teaches them that, in many situations, it is to their advantage to behave well.

- **Consequences should be appropriate**

  In some situations we can allow children to learn from natural consequences – but clearly, we would not allow them to fiddle with electrical sockets and appliances to learn about the properties of electricity.

  It would also be inappropriate to say: 'Because you bit your sister I am going to bite you.' This would model inappropriate behaviour, would cause pain and would be hurtful.

  Don't threaten the child with consequences that are way too severe – like cancelling their birthday party or making them miss a family trip to Disneyland. You will find that you either can't follow it through or, if you do, you will alienate and hurt the child. The aim of consequences is not to shame or humiliate the child. If a child appears to accept a consequence calmly this does not mean it is not having an effect. They will still learn from the experience.

  Setting logical consequences can also be quite challenging if you are the kind of carer who instinctively draws back from situations of conflict. Using the guidelines that make consequences effective can be helpful here to ensure that you can follow through. If you can't think of an appropriate consequence on the spot, you can tell the child that you need time to decide what the consequence will be.

- **Consequences need to be immediate**

  Children can't relate to consequences that are too far ahead, such as cancelling a treat the following week. They are more likely to get the message if the consequences follow quickly and they have to do something straight away or at least within 24 hours. It's best to keep consequences short and to the point, so the child can quickly get on with positive activities again. If you take the child's playdough away for five minutes because he is throwing it around, make sure he gets the chance to play with it again so that you can praise him for playing with it properly this time.

You might decide to let the child learn from certain natural consequences. For instance, if he refuses to get out of bed, he will miss the school bus. If he refuses to take his coat to school, he will get cold or wet.

- **Consequences should be straightforward**

  It's best to deliver any consequences in a calm and matter-of-fact way. Try to avoid lecturing the child, getting into arguments or listening to his protests and pleas. (Remember how attention from you will reward inappropriate behaviour.)

  Avoid being too apologetic about it ('I'm really sorry you are going to have to miss your favourite programme now') or too critical ('Well, it serves you right!'). If you let your own feelings show, they will get in the way of the child's learning and the strategy will be less effective. The idea of this strategy is that the child learns from experiencing the negative consequences of his choices, not from your displeasure.

Do you struggle with the idea of setting consequences?

You may be painfully aware that the child you are caring for may have been badly treated or harshly disciplined in his family. This sometimes makes carers feel reluctant to apply consequences for fear of causing further suffering and distress for the child.

It is good to be sensitive to the fact that a child's previous experience may affect the way they interpret a situation or experience. A child who has experienced physical abuse, for example, might be used to a raised voice being followed by violence. A child who has been emotionally abused might be more likely to feel humiliated and shamed by any reference to their shortcomings. Remember that the situation in your home is very different from that in the child's home: the consequences you set will be fair and you will apply them calmly and in the context of a caring relationship with the child – not an abusive relationship. You will, of course, ensure that any strategies you use do not infringe the child's rights or dignity.

Setting logical consequences can be quite challenging if you are the kind of carer who instinctively draws back from situations of conflict. It might help if you remind yourself of the following:

- Children need boundaries, limits and consequences even if they protest and react against them.
- Making a child face consequences when he behaves badly will help him in the long term because he will learn to behave better and there will be less conflict in his life in the future.

- It is in the child's best interests for you to be firm and consistent in applying consequences.
- Progress with some children may be slow and painful, but it is still a move in the right direction.

COMING UP WITH CONSEQUENCES

Think of some suitable logical consequences for the following behaviours and write them in the box.

Behaviour

Your child is playing dangerously on the seesaw at the playground

A possible logical consequence

___

___

Behaviour

Your child is playing roughly with a toy

A possible logical consequence

___

___

Behaviour

Your child is wandering away from you on a walk

A possible logical consequence

___

___

See below for some possible logical consequences.

Behaviour	A possible logical consequence
Your child is playing dangerously on the seesaw at the playground.	**He has to get off and sit on a bench for five minutes.**
Your child is playing roughly with a toy.	**You take the toy away for a short time (timing varies according to the age of the child) but it should be brief so that the child can have another go at playing more appropriately.**
Your child is wandering away.	**Your child has to walk with you, holding your hand, for the next few minutes.**

Using logical consequences

Here's an example of how it works:

- **Give a warning**: 'You must draw on the paper, not on the table. If you draw on the table I will put your crayons away for five minutes.'
- **If the child doesn't follow your instruction, withdraw the activity. Do it quickly. Avoid getting drawn into arguments.** 'You are drawing on the table and not on the paper, so I am putting the crayons away for five minutes.'
- **After the time has elapsed, return the activity to the child. This gives him the opportunity to play with the crayons again and do it properly this time. Make sure you praise him for drawing on the paper!**
- **If he carries on drawing on the table, take the activity away for longer.**

'No ice lolly for Sarah'

Heather was fostering three-year-old Sarah and two younger boys. She would sometimes struggle to find the best way to manage Sarah's attention-seeking behaviour.

'When I picked up the children from nursery, I would have three of them in the back of the car. Sarah would be kicking the seat or teasing the little ones, and when you're driving you can't really do anything, so I used to keep shouting at her and threatening her, saying: "You wait, when you get home you won't get that ice lolly".'

So the trips home from nursery were stressful for Heather. But after learning about logical consequences, she found a better way.

'When I collected them from nursery, I said to Sarah: "Listen, I am only going to tell you this once. While we are in the car, if you misbehave I am not going to shout at you but when we get home you will not have any sweets or ice cream".'

'She did misbehave, so when we got home I gave the boys an ice lolly but Sarah did not get one.

'She must have understood because the next time, she didn't do it again.'

CONSEQUENCES

Now think of one or two minor behaviour problems your child has that you would like to tackle. Think of a logical consequence you could apply to each of them.

Behaviour	A possible logical consequence
1	
2	

Over the next week, have a go at applying these consequences whenever necessary. Make a note of what happens, below.

DAY	BEHAVIOUR	CONSEQUENCE	COMMENTS/ OBSERVATIONS
1			
2			
3			

DAY	BEHAVIOUR	CONSEQUENCE	COMMENTS/ OBSERVATIONS
4			
5			
6			
7			

When things are not going well, remind yourself of times when you have set limits or applied consequences and the results have been positive.

Did you notice a reduction in either of the behaviours over the course of the week? Keeping good records helps us to track changes accurately – to stick with strategies that are working and change approaches that are not effective.

If you did, the consequences are proving effective.

If the problem behaviour has not reduced by the time you have applied the consequence several times, have another think about what you've been doing.

- Have you remembered to issue a warning first, so that the child has the chance to choose to stop misbehaving?
- Have you been applying the consequence immediately after the child misbehaves? Too long a gap and he won't make the connection.
- Are your logical consequences short and to the point? A consequence that is unrelated to the misbehaviour is confusing and if it takes too long it gets in the way of appropriate behaviour. Make sure the child gets back to positive activity straight after the consequence, so you can praise him for behaving well.
- Have you applied the consequence on every occasion the child has done this particular thing? If you are inconsistent, it will take him longer to learn.
- Have you been able to stay calm when you apply the consequence or have you been letting your own feelings of anger or anxiety show?
- Have you managed to avoid getting drawn into arguments with the child about the consequence? When you get into discussions with the child you are paying him extra attention – without knowing it, you could be rewarding the very behaviour that you are trying to get rid of.

11 Using "time-out"

Many looked after children have come from disrupted, chaotic, neglectful and even harmful backgrounds. They may have never experienced family life that is stable, predictable, warm and encouraging.

In Chapters 3 to 5 we explored different ways you can build up positive experiences for children and reward them for appropriate behaviour. Once children have learned that life can be more predictable and pleasant, they will not want to lose your positive attention.

"Time-out from positive and negative reinforcement" – sometimes just called "time-out" for short – means withdrawing your attention in response to misbehaviour. It is a strategy you can use with fairly serious behaviour problems.

It means time-out from your positive and negative attention. In other words, for a set period of a few minutes the child has to go to a particular place and while she is there you avoid talking to her or interacting with her in any way. Time-out must be used with sensitivity and care.

Using time-out

You may have heard the term "time-out" before – perhaps you even use a version of it yourself or you may know other carers who do. People use this term to cover a variety of different disciplinary measures. Some people use what they call "time-out" in a harsh and abusive way, sending a child up to her room and completely ignoring her for long periods, regardless of how she is behaving, but this is NOT what we mean by time-out and how we use it.

You may be concerned that time-out is not a suitable punishment for a child, especially a child who may have been neglected or abused. Time-out definitely does ***not*** mean putting the child in a secluded place or shutting or locking her in a room, and the aim emphatically is ***not*** to frighten or distress the child. Some children in foster care may have had abusive experiences of enforced isolation and confinement, and they would experience isolation as frightening or rejecting. When time-out is done properly it is not unsuitable for these children.

This chapter will show you how to use time-out appropriately, as a tool for managing difficult behaviour calmly and consistently while still respecting the child. It simply involves removing positive and negative attention for a short time. To use time-out properly, you need to understand the social learning principles behind it. It can be useful with younger children and those up to the age of 12. (With older children, problem-solving and structured consequences are likely to be more effective.)

Time-out is something carers can use instead of more negative responses like arguing, shouting, blaming and criticising. It provides time and space for both you and the child to calm down. It's not an alternative to reasoning and discussion but it can be used when conflict is mounting and talking reasonably is no longer an option for either you or the child.

What behaviour will result in time-out?

Decide on one or two behaviours that will result in time-out, for example:

- She persistently refuses to do as she is told.
- She is being destructive.
- She is being aggressive.

Only apply time-out to one or two behaviours – if you use it for too many types of misbehaviour, you may end up over-using time-out and the child will not receive enough positive attention.

Where will time-out be?

For time-out, the child should be somewhere dull, away from television and activities so there is nothing to reward and interest her. Ideally, it should be somewhere you can see her. For young children, you can put a chair by a wall or in the hallway. It should be somewhere safe, so that the child cannot cause damage to herself or property during time-out. Bedrooms are not a good idea as they are often too interesting and you don't want to create an association between the bedroom and being disciplined for bad behaviour.

How long should time-out be?

It should be brief – perhaps three minutes. However, the child should not be allowed out of time-out until she is quiet. She must be quiet in order to come out of it, even if she has screamed and protested through most of it.

You will have to decide how long she has to be quiet for before she can come out of time-out. For some children it might be two minutes – for others, half a minute.

The first time you use time-out, the child may protest and scream and shout – which means time-out may go on for 20 or 30 minutes or even longer. Children learn very quickly that the sooner they quieten down, the sooner they can come out.

Explain it to the child beforehand

The child needs to know about time-out before you use it. This needs to be done when the child is calm – not just as they are being reprimanded for breaking a rule. Explain clearly which behaviours will result in time-out and what will happen.

For example: 'We are going to practise a way to help you stop this. When you pinch or bite your brother, you will go immediately to time-out. This means I will take you to the bottom step in the hall and you will have to sit there on your own for three minutes. I will not talk to you or give you any attention while you are there. You have to sit there until you are calm and quiet and I will tell you when you can come out of time-out.' You can decide, according to the child's age, how long they need to sit calmly and quietly – this could be for 30 seconds or it could be a minute, the shorter the better. Check that she has understood by getting her to tell you what will happen.

What to do when your child misbehaves

Make sure other members of the family understand time-out and do not reward the child by paying her any attention when she is in time-out.

Explain to the child what she has done and that she has to go to time-out. When she is there, do not interact with her in any way. Ignore crying, protests and minor misbehaviour. Get on with the washing up, reading the newspaper or housework or talk to someone else.

Coping with the child's reaction

Some children are fine with time-out. Others, of course, complain, threaten, cry or use other tactics to try and get out of the situation. They may say they feel unwell, or hungry, or say things that are calculated to make you feel bad or guilty.

This can be really upsetting and you may be tempted to give in, but you mustn't – the child needs to learn that she cannot get her own way by doing or saying things like this.

These early time-out experiences can be difficult for carers to cope with. Here are some ways you can help yourself to stay strong.

- Have your partner or a friend there to support you and help distract you so that you don't give in to the child's protests.

- Be confident that, used properly, time-out will not harm the child – in the long run, this experience will benefit her because it will help her learn to behave better. It is better for both of you if you can use time-out instead of losing your temper.
- To stay calm, take deep breaths and count to 10 or repeat a positive affirmation like: 'She is going to be OK. I will remain calm and firm for her.'
- Remind yourself that the first few times will be hard – but once the child learns that you do not give in, she will calm down much more quickly when she is in time-out. She will learn that she can get out of it sooner by being co-operative.

WHAT HAPPENS AT THE END OF TIME-OUT?

At the end of time-out, this is what you do.

- After time-out, avoid telling off the child or even talking about what has happened.
- Never insist that she apologises or shows remorse. She can learn her lesson without this.
- If the child had refused to carry out an instruction, repeat the instruction until she has done what you wanted.
- Encourage the child to get involved in some positive activity.
- As soon as you can, praise the child for something or look for a chance to "attend" (see Chapter 4). This shows her that you do not bear a grudge and the conflict is over.

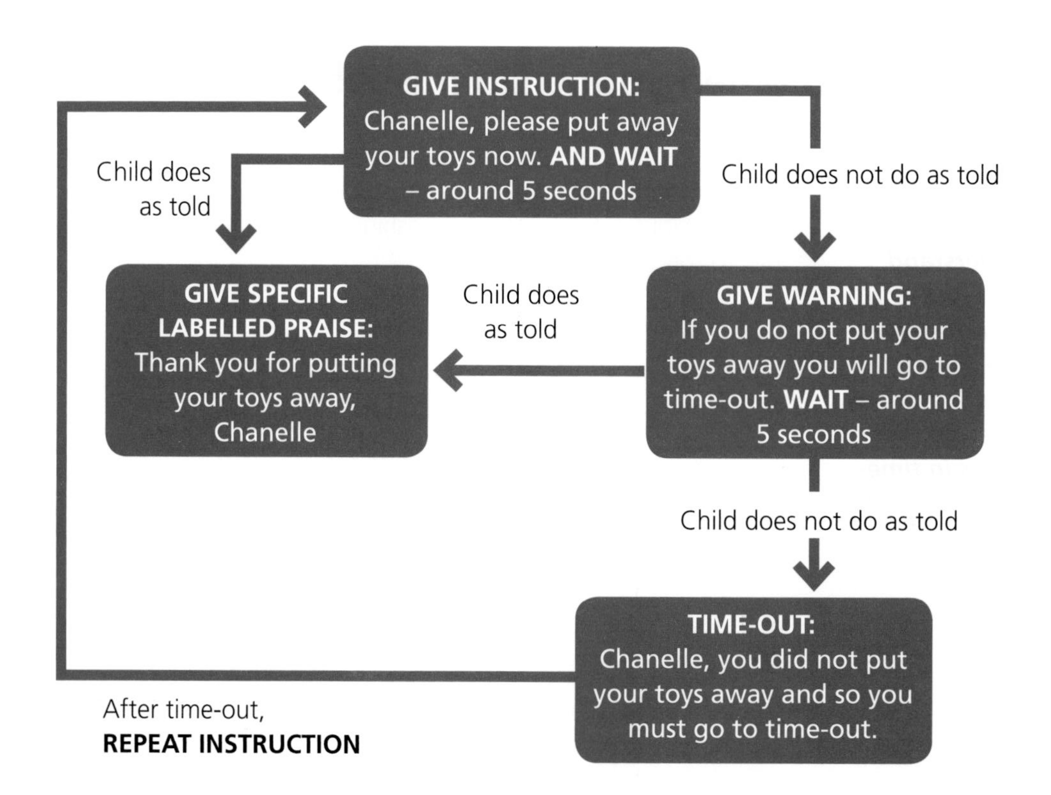

When the child does not co-operate

- **If she refuses to go to time-out**

  With a young child, you can lead her firmly to the time-out place or chair. With an older child, avoid physical contact as it may come across as aggression. Instead, add time on to the time-out period. Add one or two minutes a time, up to a total of five minutes' time-out: *As you have not done as I told you and gone into time-out, you will now have to stay in time-out for five minutes.*

  If she still won't co-operate, going over five minutes will be unproductive. In this case, warn her that you will withdraw a privilege: *If you don't go into time-out now, you won't be able to watch television for the rest of the evening.*

- **If she comes out of time-out before she is allowed to**

  With a young child, return her to the place; if you have to, stay with her there to make sure she doesn't leave it, avoid talking or making eye contact. With an older child, give a warning that you will withdraw a privilege if they don't go to time out. Ensure that it is a fairly big consequence, such as a total screen ban.

- **If she is destructive in time-out**

  Do not let her get out of time-out by being destructive. With a child who is likely to be destructive, choose a place for time-out where there is nothing valuable that she could damage. Hold her accountable for what she does – afterwards, she must clear up any mess she has made or, if she has broken something, pay for a replacement out of her own pocket money or lose a privilege.

- **If she refuses to come out of time-out**

  The child may try to turn it into a power struggle. Avoid engaging in this; instead, simply say to the child, 'Time-out is over now. If you want to sit there for longer that's fine.' Some children may need longer to calm down.

Using time-out when you are out of the house

When you become more confident with time-out, you can use it out of the house too. At a party, restaurant or on a shopping trip, make it clear how you want the child to behave. Provide incentives for good behaviour and spell out the consequences of misbehaviour. If you need to use time-out, this could be in the car, on the stairs or somewhere else away from where she wants to be. (You might need to explain what you are doing to any concerned passers-by.)

"Calm-down time" with the under-fives

With young children, it is often enough to remove them from the activity and get them to sit quietly on the edge of the activity for a minute or two. Withdraw your attention. When they have calmed down, allow them to return to the activity. *You are throwing sand around in the sandpit, so you will have to come and sit on the side for two minutes. After that, you can go back to the sandpit to play.*

Remember, time-out is just one of the strategies you can use to turn around a child's behaviour. Always look for opportunities to provide praise, warmth and positive attention – these are the things that will encourage the child to behave well, enhance her self-esteem, and strengthen the attachment between you. Try to make sure your child experiences many more positive interactions than disciplinary ones!

"CALM-DOWN TIME" FOR YOU

- **When you are getting frustrated and annoyed with a child but you recognise that the problem is with you and not her, give *yourself* some "time-out" by removing yourself from the situation.**
- **Go off into another room for a cup of tea and listen to some music or have a walk around the garden. Or talk to your partner, a friend or your link worker from the fostering agency. Do whatever helps you calm down and avoid conflict.**

Over the next few days, use the table on the next page to reflect on your experiences with time-out and track progress.

Think of one or two ways your child misbehaves that might be suitable for time-out:

When I could use time-out

1 ______________________________

2 ______________________________

3 ______________________________

Which place will you use for time-out?

____

____

____

How many minutes will time-out last?

____

____

____

How long must your child be quiet for, before being allowed out of time-out?

____

____

____

Explain time-out to your child.

My experiences with time-out

DAY AND TIME	BEHAVIOUR	WHAT HAPPENED DURING TIME-OUT	WHAT HAPPENED AFTERWARDS

You should notice:

- The child calms down sooner each time.
- The targeted misbehaviour starts to become less frequent and/or less intense when you have used time-out on several occasions.
- You feel more and more confident about using time-out.

When problems are extreme

The "non-violent resistance" approach

Your fostering agency should have issued guidelines for managing aggressive and destructive behaviour and you will, of course, discuss strategies with them if the child or young person you are caring for behaves in this way. Some young people's behaviour is extreme and they attempt to control, intimidate and use violence against their carers or other children in the household. In such cases, the child's social worker will clearly need to consider whether a foster placement is safe and appropriate. In many cases it will not be. However, there is a therapeutic approach that has proved effective for some parents and carers who are struggling with a child's or young person's violent and destructive behaviour and who desperately need to turn things around for their family.

"Non-violent resistance" (NVR) is a form of family therapy aimed at helping parents to deal effectively with their helplessness, isolation and escalatory interactions with their children. They are taught and supported to use the approach by a trained clinical psychologist or other therapist over a number of weekly sessions, with telephone support in addition.

NVR was developed as a parent training programme by Haim Omer, a professor of psychology at Tel Aviv University in Israel (Omer *et al*, 2008), and was introduced to the UK in 2006 by Dr Peter Jakob, a clinical psychologist who has developed its use with looked after children (2006a, 2006b). It is available in certain parts of the UK.

The key aspects are:

- Making a stand against the young person's violent behaviour without using physical or verbal aggression
- Preventing escalation
- Protecting the victims
- Enlisting the help of friends and relatives who can act as mediators and supporters
- Using the parents' or carers' increased presence, sometimes in the form of a "sit-in" in the child's room after a major incident
- Taking steps towards reconciliation with the child

A study (Weinblatt and Omer, 2008) that evaluated training in NVR with the parents of children with acute behavioural problems showed a decrease in escalatory behaviours and an increase in perceived social support and reported a clear improvement in the relationship between the parents and the aggressive child.

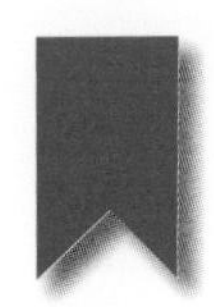

'Using time-out has helped me'

Time-out is one of the strategies Stella learned on the* Fostering Changes *course.

'When I started using time-out with Chantelle, being in her room made her angry and she would throw her toys and slam the door and cried and cried for so long. Because of how she is, time-out could go on and on and we didn't want her to spend so much time on her own in her room. So now time-out happens in our sitting room and when I say "time-out", she goes.'

12 Problem-solving

In this chapter we will look at how you can help your child develop problem-solving skills and become more skilled at making decisions.

Problem-solving may be completely unfamiliar to your child. Children who come from disorganised and chaotic families may not have learned how to resolve differences and conflict constructively, or been given the chance to make decisions. When children come into care, many decisions concerning them are made by others – this can make them feel particularly powerless. Problem-solving gives a bit of power and control back to children. It can help them develop a sense of themselves as active, confident and competent decision-makers.

Learning to problem-solve is about *how* to think, not *what* to think. It's a way of thinking about different possible solutions and finding a way forward. It's a really useful life skill for anyone to have. We talked about resilience in Chapter 1 and we know that problem-solving is a key resilience factor that helps to promote self-efficacy and, in turn, leads to increased self-esteem in children. As adults, we are often tempted to take short cuts and provide ready-made solutions for children. However, children will grow in confidence and independence if adults support and guide them in finding their own solutions to problems.

In fact, problem-solving is not just a single skill – it involves a number of different skills, such as listening to other people's viewpoints, clarifying issues, negotiating, collaborating, using empathy to see things from someone else's perspective, and keeping calm. Problem-solving can help develop children's cognitive skills as well as enhancing their social skills. So it's also about feelings – it means taking into account your own feelings and those of others.

Coaching problem-solving

Problem-solving is something you and the child can do together, so choose a time when you are both feeling relatively relaxed, positive and ready to communicate. When you first try this out, use it with a relatively straightforward problem the child has that is not too complex or emotionally charged.

The framework we use is **Stop – Plan – Go** (Stallard, 2002).

STOP

- **Think**
- **Take a deep breath in and breathe out slowly**

PLAN

- Think about what you want to do and say differently
- You may have a number of ideas – some may seem silly
- That's OK
- Choose one and imagine yourself doing it. Who can help you? What are the consequences?

GO

- **Try it out!**
- **It may not work first time. If not, revisit your plan and try another way**
- **If it works – keep doing it and think of ways to remember your plan**

WELL DONE!

STOP

What is the problem?

The first step is to stop and consider what the problem is. Suggest that the child takes a deep breath, saying "Stop". Then ask him to tell you the problem.

The "Stop" stage is a reminder to prevent children from acting without thinking or rushing into situations. This is actually one of the hardest things for children to learn. Eventually they will internalise the process and be able to say "Stop" in their heads rather than out loud. It is important that the carer discover the child's point of view about the problem rather than assuming they understand it. Carers need to hold onto to their own assumptions and concerns.

PLAN

What could you do and/or say?

This stage involves the child generating lots of possible solutions, rather than trying to find one "correct" solution. He needs to be able to think as freely and as creatively as possible – so avoid judging or criticising any of his ideas. Write them down. If there are ideas that seem silly or that you don't like, just be neutral about them. If the child really can't come up with any plan, prompt him with one or two simple ideas.

Now go through the list of ideas with him, one at a time. Identify the positive and negative consequences of each action.

The child then chooses the best one and imagines doing it.

He then prepares to put the plan into action.

GO

Put the plan into action.

It may not work first time. If it doesn't, revisit your plan and try another way. If it does – well done!

Example

STOP

The child defines the problem: *When I am in the playground, Sabrina keeps hitting me.*

PLAN

Child's suggested ideas for what to do:

- Hit her back
- Tell a teacher
- Run off
- Shout at her "Stop it!"
- Ask her why

- Hide from her at playtime
- Tell everyone something horrible about her

The child considers the possible consequences of each of these options, and decides which one to go with.

GO

The child puts his plan into action.

Some tips

- Listen rather than judging (remember your listening skills).
- Ask the child what he thinks. Encourage him to share his own ideas. Praise him for trying and for coming up with suggestions.
- Refrain from giving advice. Instead, prompt the child to come up with his own answers (in an encouraging way): *What do you think? How do you think you could find out?*
- Acknowledge how your child sees the problem. Think about it from his perspective.
- Some of the options may have short-term attraction – such as the child hitting Sabrina back – so be ready to acknowledge these and consider the disadvantages with the child. Help him consider the longer-term consequences as well as the short-term ones.
- Check things out – avoid trying to mind-read others, for example, *'If I've understood you correctly, you are saying that…'*
- He will gradually discard the solutions with less satisfactory consequences and be left with the one that he thinks is best.
- When he has chosen his course of action, help him decide where and when he will do it and rehearse what he plans to say or do. If appropriate, you could ask: *Who can help you?*
- Afterwards, encourage him to evaluate how he got on.
- Praise him for carrying out his plan, and for his problem-solving efforts, whatever the outcome.
- If it didn't work, give the child an opportunity to think about why, and to come up with some further alternative solutions.

When you have a decision to make or a problem to solve, voice your own decision-making processes out loud so that children can see how it's done. Model problem-solving skills such as using empathy and keeping calm.

Things that get in the way

Watch out for things that can get in the way of the problem-solving process. Difficulties can occur if a particular problem raises a strong critical reaction in us. At these times it is important to use a lot of self-control around our own feelings. It's harder to think clearly when we are tired, annoyed or preoccupied or emotional. Sometimes, instead of helping the child think through the problem, we might slip into negative habits like giving advice, denying the problem, placating the child, giving our own solutions, criticising or complaining.

USING STOP – PLAN – GO

Here are some examples of scenarios in which carers could use the **Stop – Plan – Go** system to resolve problems with their child. What possible solutions do you think children might come up with, and which would be the best way of resolving the problems?

- Kyle complains that you never cook any food that he likes. Use Stop – Plan – Go to think about this with Kyle.
- Carl has been rude and aggressive to William, who has just come into placement. William tends to talk non-stop and follows Carl around, wanting to play with him all the time. Carl comes to tell you how annoying he finds William. Use Stop – Plan – Go to address this problem with Carl.
- Jamila can't decide how she would like to celebrate her birthday.
- Joe is supposed to be going to football practice but it clashes with a friend's party that he is really keen to go to.

Try problem-solving with your child

Following the guidelines and tips above, do a problem-solving exercise with your child. Record this in the space below.

STOP	**What is the problem?**		
PLAN	Possible solutions	Advantages	Disadvantages
	1	1	1
	2	2	2
	3	3	3
	4	4	4
	5	5	5
	6	6	6
	The solution I have chosen:		
GO	**When and how to put my plan into action:**		

	Outcome:
	Did it work?

*Explain to the child that **Stop – Plan – Go** is like the traffic light system. If you think it will help, put a red sticker on the child's pencil case, school bag, etc, to act as a reminder to stop and think before acting.*

Using problem-solving to make group decisions

You can also use this problem-solving technique for finding solutions or making decisions about more light-hearted issues; for example, at the weekend, making a decision as to how the family are going to spend the afternoon. Using the same framework, you can all sit together, carers and children, receive all the ideas and then go through them one by one identifying pros and cons and choosing the one that gets most pros!

Using problem-solving in your own life

We all have problems to resolve and decisions to make big and small, pretty much all the time. These might be to do with managing children's behaviour or other issues concerning our own family, relationships, work, house or money. Sometimes, when we are stressed or tired, it's hard to think things through calmly and rationally. So you might find this problem-solving technique comes in handy in your own life too. Try using problem-solving for one of your own dilemmas, such as what to do this weekend. In this way you will become familiar and confident with the process before using it with your child.

13 Managing transitions and change

Transitions can be a source of excitement and stress for children and young people, whether they are moving from their foster placement to a new placement or to an adoptive family or returning home, or whether it is some other kind of transition, such as moving from primary school to secondary school.

Making endings as positive as they can be

Foster carers have a key role to play in managing the ending of a placement. When a child in your care is moving on to live elsewhere, returning home or changing schools, for example, she is likely to have mixed feelings about leaving behind her carers, her friends and others. You yourself may also have mixed emotions about it and will have to manage the child's feelings as well as your own.

Allow and encourage the child to express her feelings – sadness, worry, anger, fear, relief, excitement, happiness. Acknowledge your own feelings too. Talk about the child's achievements but also the difficulties, as well as how her behaviour has changed. You could mark the transition with a little ceremony of some kind, such as a party, taking the whole family out for a meal, or baking a cake.

Make sure the child is given as much information as possible about the new placement or the new plans – be ready to listen, talk to her about it and answer her questions.

How you can preserve memories for the child and make the transition positive

Children in care, especially those who have had a number of moves, won't be able to remember everything when they are older. Having gaps in your life story can be distressing. So preserving some of these memories for her is a really valuable thing to do for the child.

You will have witnessed key moments in her life during the time she has been with you.

With younger children, you may have witnessed the first time they spoke or learnt to walk. Many carers will have seen their children start new schools, make friends and gain new skills. If children are to develop a good sense of who they are and where they come from, they need their story to be remembered and passed on to them so that they can take this with them.

Here are a few ideas – you will probably also have some of your own.

- Recount things the child has done or said while with you.
- Make a memory box – spend some time together taking or collecting up photographs of the child's time with you, certificates she was awarded, stories she has written and so on.
- Write an account or story about the child's time with you – the day she arrived, things that happened at school, the clubs she went to, the way she played with your children or your family pet, etc. Focus on your positive feelings for the child and let her know you will always remember her. Get the child to draw the artwork.
- Record the story and give it to her so that she can listen to it and think about you thinking about her.
- Make sure she takes with him everything that she brought into the placement – even if, to you, it doesn't seem worth keeping, it may have meaning for her.
- If possible, arrange some shared activities with the child's new carers/adoptive family.
- Plan for how you and the child might stay in contact in future (if appropriate). Discuss this with the social worker. You might be able to arrange visits or keep in touch with cards, letters or emails.

Looking at the changes

Think back over the ideas and suggestions you have learned about through this training programme.

When you have thought about the concepts, completed the exercises and spent some time trying out the various strategies, think about what has changed as a result.

Try to write down three things in response to each of the questions below.

The changes I have noticed

- **How have your feelings, beliefs and attitudes changed?**

  ____

  ____

  ____

- **How has your behaviour changed?**

  ____

  ____

  ____

- **How has the child's behaviour changed?**

  ____

  ____

  ____

- **How has your relationship with the child changed?**

  ____

  ____

  ____

The skills you have learned are like a tool-bag you can draw on whenever you are facing a difficult situation. You can now select strategies to address problems with the child's behaviour – see the table above.

Whatever else you do, remember to always use the tools in Column 2 – encouraging and building self-esteem. The other strategies will only work in the context of a warm, encouraging environment with praise and positive attention.

Setting goals for change

Decide which behaviour you are concerned about and then decide how you are going to tackle it, using one or more of the strategies you have learned. You might want to focus on one of the behaviours you identified at the beginning of this programme, which you listed on page 4, or you might want to focus on something different.

Baseline skills	Encouraging and building self-esteem	Setting limits and providing consequences	Additional skills
Observation	**Praise**	**Ignoring**	**Working with thoughts and feelings**
Being clear and specific	**Attending**	**Calm clear instructions**	
ABC analysis	**Choosing alternative (target) behaviour**	**Time-out**	**"I" messages** **Mindfulness practice**
	Tangible rewards	**Family rules**	
	Reward charts	**Managing rule breaking**	
	Token rewards	**Natural consequences**	
		Logical consequences	

With this behaviour in mind, work out three goals for the coming week. Be as specific as possible. For example, suppose your child is rude and aggressive when you ask her to do something, your goals for the week might be:

Goal 1: Give clear, calm instructions.

Goal 2: Ignore rude behaviour.

Goal 3: Praise and reward her when she speaks to you nicely.

At the end of the week, write down whether or not you achieved your goals. Make a note of what went well and what didn't go so well.

	Goal	Goal achieved? Yes/No	Comments
1			
2			
3			

Tackling problem behaviours

Remember the three problem behaviours you identified on page 4? You may have already tackled them during the course of this programme. If not, now is the time.

You have learned new strategies and can choose which ones to use in different situations. Here's a three-week plan to follow:

- **Week 1:**
  Focus on Problem 1, setting yourself three goals each week, as you did in the exercise above.
- **Week 2:**
  Focus on Problem 2, setting three goals. Continue the approach you were using with Problem 1.
- **Week 3:**
  Focus on Problem 3, setting three goals. Continue your approach to Problems 1 and 2, adapting if necessary – for instance, if you are using a reward chart, you might want to set new targets for your child.
- **At the end of this period, rate the problem behaviours again, below.**

  Mark the line at the appropriate place to indicate how severe the problem is now.
- **Now compare these ratings with the ratings you gave at the beginning of the programme, on page 4. You will be able to see just how much progress you have made with your child's most challenging behaviours.**

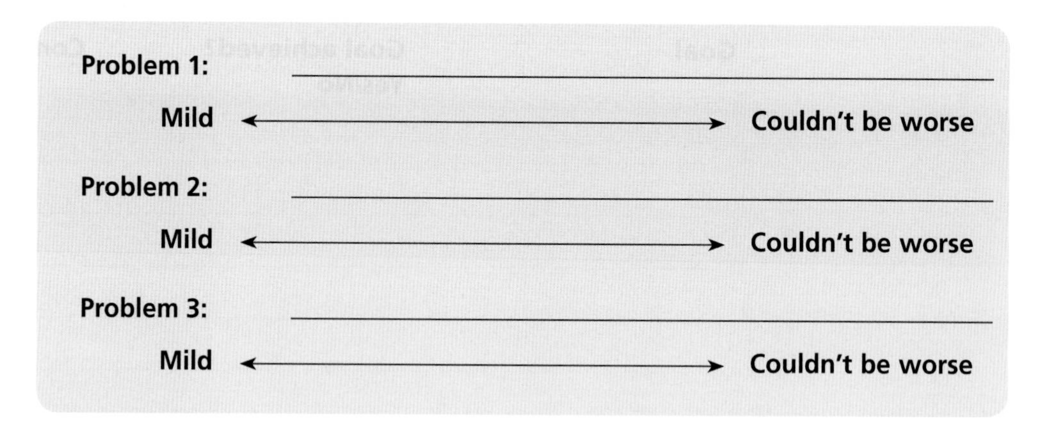

Problem 1: ______________________________

Mild ←——————————→ Couldn't be worse

Problem 2: ______________________________

Mild ←——————————→ Couldn't be worse

Problem 3: ______________________________

Mild ←——————————→ Couldn't be worse

Caring for yourself

It's great to have new behaviour management skills, but they are not enough on their own – you also need to be psychologically strong in order to look after children who may be troubled and disturbed.

Why is it important to look after yourself?

The things that create pressure in our lives can be big events, like someone being seriously ill or having an operation or a child running away, or they can be a build-up of lots of smaller events, like not being able to find things at home when your child is getting ready for school, then getting stuck in traffic and not being able to find anywhere to park, and your child being late for school.

Everyday pressures of life can lead to stress when the stressor itself hasn't changed but our resources have; for example, we might be able to cope with these things pretty well in the normal course of events but not if we are unwell or very tired. That's why it's really important for carers to care for themselves as well as their children and the children in the placement.

The stress reaction

The role of stress, and particularly stress hormones, is to prepare the body to resolve threatening situations. Stress is a physiological state, driven by adrenaline that causes the fight/flight or freeze response.

The impact of stress

Stress hormones over long periods of time impact on our physiology, our thoughts, feelings and what we do:

1. Breathing rate/heart rate and blood pressure increase
2. Blood sugar level increases
3. It lowers our immune response
4. It increases the risk of high blood pressure, depression, anxiety and stomach ulcers
5. It can cause sleep problems
6. It can make us become forgetful.

How does stress impact on the way we care for children?

Stress impacts on many of the skills that you have been developing while reading and practising the strategies in this book.

Attention: Psychology research has shown that when we experience neutral or positive emotional states we have a broader focus of attention. We are therefore able to notice the good things that our children have done and praise them. When we are experiencing negative emotions, including stress, we have a narrow focus of attention. If we are in a bad mood, everything seems bad and we will be less able to spot those little glimmers of light.

Responding to aversive behaviour: If we're feeling stressed and we have these stress hormones racing around our bodies, we are prepared for a fight/flight/freeze response. We may therefore respond in a way that shows our anger or frustration. This is a form of attention and can be reinforcing for the child.

Communication: We know that stress impacts on our thoughts, so it naturally affects what we say, but it also impacts on *how we say it*: keeping warmth and sensitivity in the tone of your voice is really important and can be lost when we feel stressed or under pressure.

Problem-solving: Psychology research again has demonstrated that when we are feeling neutral or positive emotions we are better able to problem-solve. This may mean we are better able to help our child to problem-solve, or that we ourselves can liaise successfully with school after a bad day to resolve an issue, for example.

The research: Research shows that when parents are learning parenting skills on a training course, including some input on how to handle stress leads to improved child behaviour. So parents being better able to manage their feelings really does impact on how their children behave.

Value yourself

As a carer you give to others all the time: you guide and comfort them, cuddle them, keep them healthy, well fed, busy and entertained, nurture their friendships and talents and help and support them with everything from homework to cleaning out the hamster cage. You may have to meet other people's needs too, such as those of your own parents and other family members.

It's no wonder if you sometimes feel completely drained. So it's important to spend some time on yourself – on doing the things that make you feel better, more relaxed or more energised and happier. Write down some of the things you enjoy and look forward to. It might be as simple as lying back in a bubble bath with a glossy magazine, or going for a swim (without the kids!). It might be going to a dance class or to a support group or foster carer group meeting.

You need to value yourself and make time for the things that *you* need too. Of course there will always be times when life gets in the way, but in a normal week you do need to prioritise some activities and treats that will recharge your batteries.

Write down here the time you are going to carve out for yourself in the week and what you are going to do with it.

"Me-time"	What I'm going to do with it

Remember, you have earned the right to have some pleasure, leisure and fun. And the more relaxed and happier you are, the better it is for your children. You need to look after yourself so you can look after them.

Well done!

Congratulations on completing this programme – we hope that you and your child or children are enjoying the benefits and will continue to do so for a long time to come.

References

David B and Wassell S (2002) *Assessing and Promoting Resilience in Vulnerable Children* (vols 1, 2 and 3), London: Jessica Kingsley

Fostering Network (2014) *The Skills to Foster: Handbook and leader's guide*, London: Fostering Network

Fursland E (2010) *Foster Care and Social Networking*, London: BAAF

Gilligan R (1997) 'Beyond permanence: the importance of resilience in child placement practice and planning', *Adoption & Fostering*, 21:1, pp 12–20

Goleman D (1996) *Emotional Intelligence: Why it can matter more than IQ*, London: Bloomsbury

Jakob P (2006a) 'Peace dividend', *Community Care*, June, pp 32–33

Jakob P (2006b) 'Bringing non-violent resistance to Britain', *Context,* 36: pp 38, 84

Kabat-Zinn J (2004) *Wherever you go, There you are: Mindfulness meditation for everyday life*, London: Piatkus

Omer H, Schorr-Sapir I and Weinblatt U (2008) 'Non-violent resistance and violence against siblings', *Journal of Family Therapy*, 30, pp 450–464

Schofield G and Beek M (2006) *The Attachment Handbook for Foster Care and Adoption*, London: BAAF

Schofield G and Beek M (2014) *The Secure Base Model: Promoting attachment and resilience in foster care and adoption*, London: BAAF

Stallard P (2002) *Think Good, Feel Good: A cognitive behaviour therapy workbook for children and young people*, Chichester: Wiley

Weinblatt U and Omer H (2008) 'Non-violent resistance: a treatment for parents of children with acute behavior problems', *Journal of Marital and Family Therapy*, 34, pp 75–92

Woolgar M (2013) 'The practical implications of the emerging findings in the neurobiology of maltreatment for looked after and adopted children: recognising the diversity of outcomes', *Adoption & Fostering*, 37: pp 237–252